THE CHALLENGE OF TRANSLATING TRUTH

*Bible Translation—
No Easy Matter*

EDWARD D. ANDREWS

THE CHALLENGE OF TRANSLATING TRUTH

Bible Translation—No Easy Matter

Edward D. Andrews

Christian Publishing House
Cambridge, Ohio

Copyright © 2019, 2024 Edward D. Andrews

All rights reserved. Except for brief quotations in articles, other publications, book reviews, and blogs, no part of this book may be reproduced in any manner without prior written permission from the publishers. For information, write, support@christianpublishers.org

THE CHALLENGE OF TRANSLATING TRUTH: Bible Translation —No Easy Matter by Edward D. Andrews

ISBN-10: 194958691X

ISBN-13: 978-1949586916

Table of Contents

TRANSLATIONS Referred to in this Publication 7

Preface 9

Introduction 12

SECTION ONE The Hazardous Work of the Bible Translator 17

CHAPTER 1 Bible Translation Is a Hazardous Duty 20

CHAPTER 2 The Wycliffe Bible – The Word of Our God Endures Forever 24

CHAPTER 3 The Life and Martyrdom of Bible Translator John Hus (1369-1415) 30

CHAPTER 4 The Betrayal and Death of the Translator William Tyndale 36

SECTION TWO Translation Philosophy, Process, and Differences 42

CHAPTER 5 Basics of Bible Translation 46

CHAPTER 6 Translation Philosophy 53

CHAPTER 7 The Different Kinds of Bible Translations 60

CHAPTER 8 The Making of a Worthy Translation 67

SECTION THREE Translation Principles 73

CHAPTER 9 Idioms in Bible Translation 78

CHAPTER 10 Translating the Unknown 87

CHAPTER 11 Translating Special Terms 93

CHAPTER 12 Translating Things that Get in the Way of Understanding 99

SECTION FOUR Translation Choices that Are Not Easy to Make 103

CHAPTER 13 Gender-Inclusive Language in Bible Translation 106

CHAPTER 14 John 8:58 Why Should the Bible Translator Be Faithful So as to Give the Reader What God Said.......................... 111

CHAPTER 15 Acts 20:28 To What and to Whom Should a Good Bible Translation Be Faithful?.. 115

CHAPTER 16 Romans 9:5 Why Are Translation Choices No Easy Matter?... 120

CHAPTER 17 Titus 2:13 and 2 Peter 1:1 What is the Long-Debated Controversial Granville Sharp Rule? 125

CHAPTER 18 John 2:4 Was Jesus Disrespectful to His Mother?.. 129

CHAPTER 19 Mark 10:15 Over and Under Translation of the Bible... 132

SECTION FIVE: The Reliability of Our Bibles 136

CHAPTER 20 The Author's Intended Meaning Should Not Always Be Immediately Clear... 140

CHAPTER 21 Why Have Modern Bible Translation Removed Words, Phrases, Sentences, Even Whole Verses? 143

CHAPTER 22 Mistakes Were Made in Copying God's Word, But Was the Purity of the Bible Text Threatened? Were These Serious Enough to Ruin the Message of the Bible? 148

CHAPTER 23 How the Bible Survived Careless and Even Deceitful Bible Copyists?... 158

Bibliography... 162

TRANSLATIONS Referred to in this Publication

Unless otherwise indicated, Scripture quotations are from the *Updated American Standard Version of the Holy Scriptures,* 2016 (UASV). Abbreviations used to designate other translations of the Bible are provided below:

ASV: American Standard Version (1901)

AMP: Amplified Bible (1987)

AT: The Bible – An American Translation (1935)

CEB: Common English Bible (2011)

CEV: Contemporary English Version (1995)

DARBY: Darby Translation (1890)

ERV: Easy to Read Version (2012)

GW: GOD'S WORD Translation (1995)

GNT: Good News Translation (1992)

HCSB: Holman Christian Standard Bible (2003)

JB: The Jerusalem Bible (1966)

JP: The Holy Scriptures According to the Masoretic Text (1917)

KJV: King James Version (1611, 1942)

LEB: Lexham English Bible (LEB)

LXX: Greek Septuagint Version of Hebrew Old Testament (280-150 B.C.E.)

NCV: New Century Version (2005)

NEB: New English Bible (1970)

NLV: New Life Version (1969)

NLT: New Living Translation (2013)

NTB: A New Translation of the Bible (1934)

NASB: New American Standard Bible (1995)

NET: New English Translation (2006) Biblical Studies Press

NIV: New International Version (2011)

NIVI: New International Version Inclusive Language Edition (1996)

NKJV: New King James Version (1982)

NLT: New Living Translation (2007)

NLV: New Language Version (1969)

NRSV: New Revised Standard Version (1989)

PHILIPS: New Testament in Modern English (1958)

REB: Revised English Bible (1989)

RSV: Revised Standard Version (1971)

SEB: Simple English Bible (1980)

TEB: The Emphasized Bible (1897)

TEV: Today's English Version (1976)

TLB: The Living Bible (1971)

TNIV: Today's New International Version (2005)

UASV: Updated American Standard Version (2022)

WHNU: Westcott-Hort Greek New Testament / Nestle-Aland Greek New Testament, United Bible Society Greek New Testament (1881, 2012, 1993)

YLT: Young's Literal Translation (1887)

Preface

Objective of This Publication

The Bible, as the inspired Word of God, holds a unique place in the hearts of millions. It is a source of spiritual guidance, moral instruction, and profound wisdom. Translating this sacred text into the languages of the world is a task of monumental importance and complexity. This publication, *The Challenge of Translating Truth: Bible Translation—No Easy Matter*, seeks to explore the intricacies and challenges faced by Bible translators throughout history and in contemporary times.

The objective of this work is to provide a thorough examination of the principles, philosophies, and practices that underpin faithful Bible translation. It aims to equip readers with a deeper understanding of the rigorous processes involved in rendering the original Hebrew, Aramaic, and Greek texts into accurate and readable translations in modern languages. This publication underscores the necessity of a literal translation philosophy, emphasizing that the translator's primary duty is to convey what God said through His human authors—not to interpret what the translator thinks God meant.

The introduction sets the stage by addressing the fundamental challenges of ambiguity, idioms, cultural expressions, names, titles, textual variants, and theological terms that translators must navigate. It highlights the delicate balance between literal accuracy and readability, the importance of footnotes and marginal notes, and the ethical responsibilities of translators. Additionally, it touches on the crucial task of promoting biblical literacy and addressing common misinterpretations and misconceptions.

Section One delves into the hazardous work of early Bible translators like John Wycliffe and William Tyndale, who faced immense persecution for their commitment to making the Scriptures accessible to the common people. It traces the historical context and legacy of these pioneers, demonstrating their unwavering dedication to literal translation and the enduring impact of their work.

Section Two focuses on translation philosophy, process, and differences. It provides a comprehensive overview of the foundational elements of Bible translation, including the original languages of the Bible, the importance of literal translation, the translation process, textual criticism, linguistic analysis, and the role of translation committees. It contrasts the pitfalls of functional equivalence with the case for formal equivalence and addresses common objections to literal translation.

Section Three outlines the principles that guide faithful translation, examining idioms, cultural references, theological terms, and strategies for overcoming barriers to understanding. It includes case studies and examples that illustrate the ethical responsibility of translators and the necessity of maintaining a balance between readability and accuracy.

Section Four, "Translation Choices That Are Not Easy to Make," explores the contemporary challenges faced by literal translators in a world that often favors dynamic equivalence. It highlights the pressures and opposition translators encounter and reaffirms the importance of fidelity to the original text despite these challenges.

Section Five discusses the reliability of our Bibles. It provides an overview of the integrity of the original manuscripts, the process of textual transmission, and the role of literal translations in preserving the accuracy and purity of the Bible text. It addresses common concerns and misconceptions about the trustworthiness of modern translations.

The chapters that follow delve deeper into specific translation issues, including gender-inclusive language, the Granville Sharp Rule, and the interpretation of challenging passages such as John 8:58 and Acts 20:28. They also explore the complexities of translating idioms, special terms, and obscure references. These chapters illustrate the meticulous care required to ensure that translations remain faithful to the original text and convey its intended meaning without alteration or misinterpretation.

This publication also includes an exploration of the historical context of textual transmission, the impact of variants, and the role of early Church Fathers and the Masoretes in preserving the text. It addresses both intentional and unintentional changes made by copyists and considers the theological implications of these variants.

In compiling this work, we aim to honor the legacy of faithful translators who have dedicated their lives to preserving the accuracy and integrity of the Scriptures. Their commitment serves as both an inspiration and a reminder of the sacred duty entrusted to those who undertake the task of Bible translation. We hope this publication will provide readers with a deeper appreciation of the complexities involved in translating the Bible and a renewed commitment to the principles of accuracy and faithfulness in conveying God's Word.

Edward D. Andrews

Author of 220+ books and the Chief Translator of the Updated American Standard Version.

Edward D. Andrews

Introduction

Translating the Bible is a complex and demanding task that involves preserving the divine message while making it accessible to modern readers. This chapter addresses some of the common challenges faced in Bible translation and underscores the importance of a literal translation philosophy. Our commitment is to provide readers with what God said through His human authors, ensuring the text remains faithful to the original. The meaning of a word is the responsibility of the interpreter, not the translator—**Truth Matters!**

The Challenge of Ambiguity

Ambiguity in the original texts is one of the primary challenges translators face. Biblical Hebrew and Greek often contain words or phrases that can be interpreted in multiple ways. A literal translation philosophy addresses this challenge by preserving the ambiguity, allowing readers to explore the various possible meanings.

For example, the Hebrew word *ruach* can mean "wind," "spirit," or "breath." A literal translation retains this ambiguity, allowing the context to guide the reader's understanding. Similarly, the Greek word *logos* can mean "word," "reason," or "principle." Preserving these nuances respects the original text's richness and depth.

Dealing with Idioms and Cultural Expressions

Biblical languages are replete with idioms and cultural expressions that do not have direct equivalents in modern languages. Translators must decide how to handle these phrases without losing their original meaning. A literal translation approach aims to retain the idiomatic expressions while providing footnotes or marginal notes to explain their significance.

For instance, the Hebrew idiom "to lift the face" means to show favor. Instead of replacing it with a contemporary equivalent, a literal translation would retain the phrase and explain its meaning. This approach maintains the cultural integrity of the text and enriches the reader's understanding.

Translating Names and Titles

Names and titles in the Bible carry significant theological and cultural weight. Translating these names literally preserves their original meaning and significance. For example, the name *Immanuel* means "God with us." A literal translation retains the name *Immanuel* and explains its meaning, preserving both theological depth and historical context.

Similarly, the Tetragrammaton (JHVH) should be rendered as **Jehovah** in Old Testament verses where it appears, maintaining the distinctiveness of God's name. This practice respects the sacred nature of the divine name and its importance in the Hebrew Scriptures.

Addressing Textual Variants

Textual variants pose a significant challenge in Bible translation. These variants arise from differences among ancient manuscripts. Textual criticism helps identify the most likely original reading, but translators must decide how to handle these differences in the text.

A literal translation philosophy incorporates textual variants by including footnotes that indicate alternative readings. This practice ensures transparency and allows readers to see the evidence behind the translation choices. For example, in 1 John 5:7–8, a literal translation would include a note about the Comma Johanneum, acknowledging its absence in most Greek manuscripts.

Balancing Literal Accuracy with Readability

One of the criticisms of literal translation is that it can be difficult to read. However, this challenge can be addressed without sacrificing accuracy. Translators can ensure readability by paying careful attention to grammar, punctuation, and syntax while maintaining fidelity to the original text.

For example, translators can use contemporary language structures while preserving the original wording. This approach maintains the text's integrity while making it more accessible to modern readers. Additionally, supplementary materials such as glossaries and commentaries can aid comprehension without altering the text itself.

Handling Theological Terms

Theological terms in the Bible carry profound significance and should be translated with precision. A literal translation philosophy ensures that key theological terms are rendered consistently, preserving their meaning across different contexts.

For instance, the Greek term *dikaiosynē* is often translated as "righteousness" or "justice." A literal translation would maintain this term consistently, allowing readers to trace its theological implications throughout the New Testament. This practice prevents doctrinal distortions and ensures a coherent theological message.

Dealing with Poetic and Literary Forms

The Bible contains various literary forms, including poetry, prophecy, narrative, and wisdom literature. Each form presents unique challenges for translators. A literal translation philosophy respects these forms by preserving their structure and style.

For example, Hebrew poetry often features parallelism, where the second line reinforces or contrasts with the first. A literal translation maintains this structure, allowing readers to appreciate the literary artistry. Similarly, prophetic literature contains symbolic language and imagery that should be retained to preserve its prophetic impact.

The Role of Footnotes and Marginal Notes

Footnotes and marginal notes play a crucial role in literal translations by providing additional context and explanations without altering the text. These tools help address challenges such as idioms, cultural expressions, and textual variants, enhancing the reader's understanding.

For example, a footnote can explain the significance of the Hebrew term *ḥesed*, often translated as "loving-kindness" or "steadfast love." By providing additional information, footnotes and marginal notes support the reader's engagement with the text while preserving its literal accuracy.

The Translator's Ethical Responsibility

Translators have an ethical responsibility to convey the original text faithfully. This responsibility requires rigorous scholarship, linguistic expertise, and a commitment to truth. Translators must resist the temptation to simplify or reinterpret the text, allowing it to speak for itself.

Scholarly Rigor: Translators must engage in meticulous research and analysis, ensuring their work is grounded in the best available manuscript evidence and linguistic scholarship.

Linguistic Precision: A deep understanding of the original languages is essential for accurate translation. Translators must be proficient in the nuances and subtleties of Hebrew, Aramaic, and Greek.

Commitment to Truth: Above all, translators must be committed to conveying what God said through His human authors—not what they think He meant. This commitment involves resisting interpretation and allowing the Scriptures to speak for themselves.

Addressing Misinterpretations and Misconceptions

Misinterpretations and misconceptions often arise from translations that prioritize readability over accuracy. A literal translation philosophy addresses this issue by providing a faithful rendering of the text, allowing readers to engage with the original words and meanings.

For example, the phrase "Son of Man" used by Jesus in the Gospels has deep theological implications. A literal translation retains this phrase, allowing readers to explore its significance in the context of Jesus' identity and mission. By maintaining the original wording, literal translations prevent doctrinal distortions and promote a more accurate understanding of Scripture.

Promoting Biblical Literacy

Promoting biblical literacy is essential for helping readers navigate the complexities of a literal translation. Educational resources, study guides, and Bible study programs can equip readers to understand and apply the Scriptures accurately.

For instance, a Bible study program that focuses on the historical-grammatical method of interpretation can help readers engage with the text in its original context. This approach encourages a deeper understanding of the Scriptures and fosters a commitment to truth and accuracy.

Conclusion

Translating the Bible involves numerous challenges that require careful attention and a commitment to preserving the integrity of the text. A literal translation philosophy addresses these challenges by prioritizing fidelity to the original words and structures, allowing readers to engage directly with God's Word.

SECTION ONE The Hazardous Work of the Bible Translator

The task of translating the Bible has been fraught with peril since its inception. From the days of the Septuagint (280 to 150 B.C.E.), when translators rendered the Hebrew Old Testament books into Greek, to the modern era, translators have faced significant risks. Their mission to bring the Word of God to the common languages of mankind has often been met with fierce opposition. This opposition has sometimes come from religious institutions themselves, leading to the suffering and martyrdom of many dedicated translators.

Early Translations and Their Challenges

The history of Bible translation is replete with stories of bravery and dedication. One of the earliest and most notable translations is the Septuagint. This translation of the Hebrew Scriptures into Greek was a monumental task undertaken by seventy-two scholars, according to tradition. The Septuagint was not merely a linguistic exercise but a spiritual endeavor to make the Scriptures accessible to Greek-speaking Jews dispersed throughout the Hellenistic world.

However, the road to translating the Bible was never smooth. Translators often faced hostility from those who feared the dissemination of the Scriptures in vernacular languages. This fear was rooted in the belief that laypeople interpreting the Bible for themselves could lead to heresy and a loss of control by religious authorities.

John Wycliffe and the First English Bible

In the late fourteenth century, John Wycliffe—often called the "Morning Star of the Reformation"—took on the formidable task of translating the Bible into English. Wycliffe's translation was based on the Latin Vulgate rather than the original Hebrew and Greek texts. Despite this, his work was revolutionary, making the Scriptures accessible to ordinary English-speaking people for the first time.

Wycliffe's efforts were met with intense opposition from the Church. Both Wycliffe and his followers, known as Lollards, faced severe persecution. The Church condemned his translation, and after his death, his remains were exhumed and burned as a posthumous punishment. Nevertheless, Wycliffe's translation laid the groundwork for future English translations and inspired a movement toward making the Bible available to all.

William Tyndale: A Martyr for the Word of God

The sixteenth century saw the emergence of William Tyndale, a scholar whose work would significantly impact the English Bible. Unlike Wycliffe, Tyndale translated directly from the original Hebrew and Greek texts. His New Testament, printed in 1526, was the first English translation to be produced using the printing press, allowing for broader dissemination.

Tyndale faced relentless persecution from the English Church. His translations were burned, and he was forced to flee to the Continent to continue his work. Despite the constant threat to his life, Tyndale persisted, driven by his conviction that every Englishman should have access to the Scriptures. Betrayed by a supposed friend, Tyndale was arrested, imprisoned, and eventually executed in 1536. His last words reportedly were, "Lord, open the King of England's eyes."

Tyndale's legacy is profound. His translation formed the basis for the King James Version, and his linguistic choices still influence modern English Bible translations. Tyndale's dedication and sacrifice underscore the hazardous nature of Bible translation.

The Continuing Struggle

The work of Bible translation did not become easier in the centuries that followed. Translators continued to face opposition from both religious and political authorities. The aim was always to control the interpretation of the Scriptures and to prevent what was seen as unauthorized or heretical readings.

The Geneva Bible, produced by English Protestant exiles in Geneva, Switzerland, in the 1560s, is another example of the challenges faced by translators. It was the first Bible to add numbered verses to each chapter, making it easier to reference specific passages. Despite its scholarly rigor, the Geneva Bible was viewed with suspicion by both the Church of England and the monarchy because of its marginal notes, which were seen as promoting Puritanism.

Modern Bible Translation

Today, Bible translators face different but no less significant challenges. The proliferation of English Bible translations can confuse new Bible students. With over fifty different translations available, each claiming to be the most accurate or easiest to understand, choosing the right one can be daunting. Moreover, translators must navigate the pressures of producing a text that is both faithful to the original languages and accessible to contemporary readers.

The dynamic equivalent or thought-for-thought translation philosophy, which seeks to convey the meaning rather than the exact wording of the original text, often clashes with the literal translation philosophy. The latter aims to stay as close as possible to the original words and sentence structure, trusting the reader to interpret the meaning. This ongoing debate highlights the complexities involved in Bible translation and the importance of adhering to a translation philosophy that prioritizes accuracy and faithfulness to the original text.

Conclusion

The hazardous work of Bible translators throughout history illustrates the immense sacrifices made to ensure that God's Word is accessible to all. From the early efforts of the Septuagint translators to the martyrdom of Tyndale, the history of Bible translation is one of courage, dedication, and unwavering faith. Today, as we benefit from the fruits of their labor, we must continue to uphold the principles of accuracy and faithfulness in translation, ensuring that future generations receive the unaltered truth of the Scriptures.

CHAPTER 1 Bible Translation Is a Hazardous Duty

Translating the Bible has long been a perilous endeavor, fraught with opposition, danger, and sacrifice. From the earliest translations to the modern day, those who have undertaken this sacred task have often faced severe risks. Their mission has always been to render God's Word accurately and faithfully, preserving the original intent and meaning conveyed through the human authors inspired by Jehovah.

The Early Efforts: Septuagint and Beyond

The hazardous nature of Bible translation can be traced back to the creation of the Septuagint between 280 and 150 B.C.E. This Greek translation of the Hebrew Scriptures was produced by seventy-two Jewish scholars in Alexandria. Their work was essential for Greek-speaking Jews living throughout the Hellenistic world, providing access to their sacred Scriptures in a language they understood.

However, the translation of the Scriptures was never just a scholarly task. It was a spiritually significant mission often met with fierce resistance. Many religious authorities feared the implications of making the Bible accessible in vernacular languages. They viewed such accessibility as a threat to their control over its interpretation and teaching.

John Wycliffe: The Morning Star of the Reformation

In the late fourteenth century, John Wycliffe undertook the monumental task of translating the Bible into English. His work was revolutionary in that it gave English-speaking laypeople their first opportunity to read the Scriptures for themselves. Wycliffe's translation was based on the Latin Vulgate rather than the original

Hebrew and Greek texts, but it nonetheless marked a significant step toward accessibility for the common people.

Wycliffe and his followers, known as the Lollards, faced fierce persecution for their efforts. The Church condemned his work, and after his death, Wycliffe's remains were exhumed and burned as a posthumous punishment. Despite such opposition, his translation laid the foundation for future English versions and inspired a broader movement to make the Bible available to all.

William Tyndale: A Martyr for the Word

In the sixteenth century, William Tyndale emerged as a scholar whose translation efforts had an enduring impact on the English Bible. Unlike Wycliffe, Tyndale translated directly from the original Hebrew and Greek texts. His New Testament, printed in 1526, was the first English translation produced using the printing press, making widespread distribution possible.

Tyndale faced relentless persecution from the English Church. His translations were publicly burned, and he was forced to flee England to continue his work. Betrayed by a supposed friend, Tyndale was arrested, imprisoned, and eventually executed in 1536. His last recorded words were, "Lord, open the King of England's eyes."

Tyndale's legacy is foundational. His translation formed the basis for the King James Version, and many of his linguistic decisions continue to shape modern English Bible translations. His dedication and sacrifice underscore the dangerous nature of faithfully translating the Scriptures.

The Geneva Bible: A Testament of Perseverance

The Geneva Bible, produced in the 1560s by English Protestant exiles in Geneva, Switzerland, stands as another example of the difficulties faced by Bible translators. It was the first English Bible to include numbered verses in each chapter, aiding in precise referencing. Despite its scholarly excellence, the Geneva Bible was viewed with suspicion by both the Church of England and the monarchy due to its marginal notes, which were seen as promoting Puritanism.

Modern Bible Translation: New Challenges, Same Commitment

Although physical danger is no longer the norm, modern translators face challenges of a different kind. The sheer number of English Bible versions—more than fifty—has created confusion among new Bible readers. Each version claims to be either the most accurate or the easiest to understand, making it difficult to discern which one truly adheres to the original texts.

A significant issue today is the ongoing debate between two translation philosophies: dynamic equivalence (thought-for-thought) and literal translation (formal equivalence). Dynamic equivalence seeks to convey the perceived meaning of a passage, while literal translation aims to reproduce the exact words and grammatical structures of the original languages. The latter respects the integrity of the original text and leaves interpretation to the reader, as it should be.

The Perils of Misinterpretation and Alteration

One of the greatest hazards in Bible translation is the temptation to interpret rather than translate. The role of the translator is not to explain what God meant, but to present what God, through His human authors, actually said. Interpretive translations—though often easier to read—risk introducing theological or doctrinal distortions. The translator's responsibility is to preserve the original text's integrity so that readers can engage with it and form their understanding based on what is actually written.

Commitment to Literal Translation

A literal translation philosophy is the most faithful method for conveying the original biblical text. This approach respects the historical and grammatical context of Scripture and ensures the preservation of its specific wording. Although it may at times result in a more complex reading experience, the literal method provides the most accurate rendering of God's Word.

Literal translations serve as a vital bridge between the ancient biblical languages and the modern reader, retaining the depth, nuance, and richness of the original texts. This method allows for the faithful transmission of the inspired message across languages and centuries.

The Legacy of Faithful Translators

The history of Bible translation is a story of courage, dedication, and unwavering faith. From the early work of the Septuagint scholars to the martyrdom of Tyndale, those who have labored to bring the Scriptures into the hands of ordinary people have faced considerable adversity. Their sacrifices have made it possible for generations of readers to access the Word of God.

Today, the responsibility remains. Translators must continue to uphold the principles of accuracy, integrity, and faithfulness. By doing so, they honor the legacy of those who gave their lives for this mission and ensure that the unaltered truth of the Scriptures is passed on to future generations.

Bible translation is not merely a scholarly task; it is a sacred duty. It demands courage, devotion, and a steadfast commitment to truth. As we reflect on the perilous journey of past translators, we are reminded of the immense responsibility borne by those who safeguard the Scriptures and of our duty to ensure that God's Word remains uncorrupted and accessible to all.

CHAPTER 2 The Wycliffe Bible – The Word of Our God Endures Forever

The history of Bible translation is marked by the unwavering dedication and sacrifice of those determined to make God's Word available to all people. Among the earliest and most significant of these efforts is the work of John Wycliffe, whose translation of the Bible into English in the fourteenth century remains a monumental achievement. Despite fierce opposition and persecution, Wycliffe's work laid a critical foundation for future translations and revealed the enduring power of the Scriptures.

John Wycliffe: The Morning Star of the Reformation

Born around 1330 in England, John Wycliffe was a Catholic priest and professor of theology at Oxford University. He held a firm belief that the Bible should be accessible to every person. Convinced that Scripture was the supreme authority for Christians, Wycliffe maintained that all people—regardless of education or social class—ought to read and understand the Bible for themselves. This belief directly challenged the Church's monopoly over biblical interpretation.

Wycliffe's English translation of the Bible was based on the Latin Vulgate, the standard Bible of the Church at that time. Though it was not rendered from the original Hebrew and Greek texts, the translation was a significant step toward Scripture accessibility for the English-speaking population. Wycliffe's work shattered the barrier that had kept God's Word hidden in an unfamiliar language, tightly controlled by the clergy.

Opposition and Persecution

Wycliffe's translation drew swift and fierce opposition from Church leaders, who saw vernacular Scripture as a threat to their authority. His work and teachings were condemned. His followers—known as the Lollards—were subjected to severe persecution. The Church feared that allowing the common people to read the Bible would undermine clerical control and lead to dissent.

In 1408, the Constitutions of Oxford, enacted by Archbishop Thomas Arundel, formally prohibited the translation of Scripture into English without Church authorization. This was a direct attempt to suppress Wycliffe's work. After Wycliffe's death in 1384, the Church posthumously declared him a heretic. His remains were exhumed and burned in 1428, and his ashes were scattered in the River Swift—a symbolic attempt to erase his influence. Yet his legacy endured.

The Wycliffe Bible: A Testament to Endurance

Wycliffe's translation, completed around 1382, was the first complete Bible in English. It included both the Old and New Testaments, and it was translated in a word-for-word fashion from the Latin Vulgate. While the English produced was often clumsy or awkward by modern standards, it reflected a commitment to literal accuracy based on the available source text.

These translations were copied entirely by hand, a painstaking and time-consuming process. Yet despite the dangers involved in copying, reading, or possessing the Wycliffe Bible, nearly 200 manuscripts have survived—proof of its widespread use and enduring value. The very existence of these surviving copies is a testament to the fervent desire of the English-speaking laity to know God's Word for themselves.

John Purvey and the Revision of the Wycliffe Bible

Following Wycliffe's death, his colleague John Purvey revised the translation to improve its clarity while preserving its fidelity to the Latin source. Completed around 1388, the revised version offered a more polished and accessible English text. Purvey also outlined his translation principles in the "General Prologue," where he argued that a translator must translate according to the meaning of the sentence rather than adhering rigidly to word-for-word renderings when the result would obscure the meaning. However, even then, he remained committed to the text's integrity.

Purvey wrote:

"The best translating out of Latin into English is to translate after the sentence, and not only after the words, so that the sentence be as open or opener in English as in Latin, and go not far from the letter. And if the letter may not be followed in the translating, let the sentence be ever whole and open, for the words ought to serve the intent and sentence, or else the words be superfluous or false."

Even in this explanation, we see a strong reverence for the original text. Purvey's revision was not interpretive but was designed to enhance comprehension without compromising faithfulness.

The Enduring Impact of Wycliffe's Work

Despite vigorous efforts by the Church to suppress Wycliffe's translation, it spread widely throughout England. The Lollards were instrumental in this, traveling on foot to distribute copies and read the Scriptures aloud to those unable to read. Many of them were arrested, imprisoned, or executed for possessing or spreading the Bible in English, but their commitment ensured that Wycliffe's work survived.

Wycliffe's translation had a lasting influence on the trajectory of English Bible translation. It directly inspired later translators, especially William Tyndale, who translated from the original Hebrew and Greek. Though Wycliffe's Bible relied on the Latin Vulgate, his guiding principle—that all people should have access to the Scriptures—laid the foundation for the Reformation's emphasis on sola scriptura, the authority of Scripture alone.

A Legacy of Faithfulness to the Text

Wycliffe's efforts stand as a powerful reminder of the enduring power of God's Word and the necessity of remaining faithful to the original text. While his work was imperfect, based as it was on a secondary source, his commitment to literal translation within those constraints reflected an unwavering desire to preserve and share the truth of Scripture.

As Isaiah 40:8 declares, "The word of our God endures forever." Wycliffe's translation gave voice to that enduring truth in the English tongue, despite the hostility of religious authorities. He believed that the Scriptures should not be locked behind Latin, reserved only for clerics. He believed in the power of the Bible to speak directly to every believer.

The Importance of Literal Translation

Wycliffe's commitment to a literal translation philosophy, though constrained by his use of the Latin Vulgate, still served the goal of preserving the original message. In contrast, interpretive or paraphrastic translations risk substituting the translator's thoughts for what the text actually says. The literal method remains the most honest and respectful approach to rendering the Bible, recognizing that the meaning must be discovered, not rewritten.

Even when refining difficult constructions for readability, the goal must be to transmit the original message, not to reshape it. Wycliffe's example reminds us of this balance—staying close to the words while striving to maintain clarity without intruding interpretation.

The Translation Process and Its Challenges

Bible translation demands a deep understanding of the original languages and their context. Although Wycliffe worked from a Latin version, he approached the task with reverence and meticulous care. He worked to preserve as much accuracy as possible, and the result was a faithful, if imperfect, rendering that transformed English religious life.

Challenges abound for translators: ambiguous terms, idioms, theological vocabulary, and syntax that does not neatly map from one language to another. Yet these challenges must never be a license to paraphrase or simplify in a way that redefines the text. Wycliffe's approach—copying carefully and distributing despite opposition—was driven by the view that the Scriptures belonged to God and must be made available to His people without distortion.

Perseverance in the Face of Opposition

The Church's condemnation of Wycliffe's Bible was rooted in fear—fear that the laity, reading for themselves, would question corrupt practices, challenge unscriptural traditions, and realize how far the Church had drifted from Scripture. But despite imprisonment, excommunication, and execution, Wycliffe's movement endured.

The bravery of those who risked everything to read or distribute Wycliffe's Bible testifies to the preciousness of the Word of God. It also demonstrates the lengths to which men and women of faith will go to ensure that truth is preserved and proclaimed, even when institutions oppose it.

The Lollard Movement

The Lollards, Wycliffe's followers, played a crucial role in carrying forward his legacy. They preached from the Scriptures, read the English Bible in public, and traveled from village to village despite the constant threat of arrest. Their goal was simple but bold: to bring the unfiltered Word of God to ordinary people.

Though the Lollards were persecuted mercilessly, their legacy endured. They prepared the soil for later reformers and helped to instill a growing conviction that the Bible belonged not to the hierarchy, but to every believer. Their persistence ensured the survival and continued influence of the Wycliffe Bible.

The Impact on the English Language and Culture

Wycliffe's translation shaped not only the Church but the English language itself. His use of English in the Bible gave legitimacy and structure to the developing Middle English dialects. He introduced biblical vocabulary into the vernacular and gave ordinary Englishmen the tools to discuss theology, morality, and the nature of God.

By shaping how the Bible sounded in English, Wycliffe's work influenced how English came to express abstract and spiritual concepts. His Bible laid a foundation upon which the language of later translations—especially Tyndale's and the King James Version—was built.

The Enduring Legacy of John Wycliffe

Wycliffe's legacy endures because his vision was rooted in truth. His belief that the Bible must be accessible to all people still drives faithful Bible translation today. He saw the danger of allowing institutions to interpret Scripture on behalf of the people. His conviction—that truth must be translated, not interpreted—remains relevant in every generation.

His efforts inspired later reformers who carried forward the work of translation with renewed resolve and access to better manuscripts. Wycliffe may not have lived to see the full impact of his labor, but history has rightly honored his contribution to the cause of biblical truth.

CHAPTER 3 The Life and Martyrdom of Bible Translator John Hus (1369-1415)

The story of John Hus is a profound testament to courage, conviction, and the cost of remaining faithful to the truth of God's Word. As a reformer, preacher, and early advocate for making the Scriptures accessible to the common people, Hus stands as a forerunner to the Reformation. His life, teaching, and martyrdom illuminate the perilous path walked by those committed to preserving and proclaiming the authority of the Bible over ecclesiastical tradition.

Early Life and Education

John Hus was born in 1369 in the small village of Husinec in southern Bohemia. From modest beginnings, he rose to prominence through academic achievement and spiritual devotion. He attended the University of Prague, earning his Bachelor of Arts in 1393 and Master of Arts in 1396. Known for his intellectual rigor and piety, Hus became a professor and later dean at the university, as well as an ordained Catholic priest.

It was during his academic and theological studies that Hus encountered the writings of John Wycliffe. Wycliffe's views, particularly regarding the authority of Scripture and the need for vernacular Bible translation, deeply influenced Hus. He came to believe that the Church had departed from biblical teaching and that reform was urgently needed. Central to Hus's convictions was the principle that all believers should have direct access to the Scriptures in their own language.

Preaching and Reform Efforts

Hus's reform efforts gained momentum when he became rector of Bethlehem Chapel in Prague in 1402. Bethlehem Chapel was unique in its commitment to preaching in the Czech language. There, Hus delivered powerful sermons that called the people back to the authority of the Bible and exposed the moral failings and doctrinal errors of the Church hierarchy.

He publicly denounced the sale of indulgences, the worldliness of the clergy, and the Church's growing reliance on traditions that contradicted Scripture. Like Wycliffe, Hus held that the Scriptures, not the Church, were the final authority in matters of faith. He argued that Christ alone was the Head of the Church and that the Pope and Church councils were subject to the Word of God.

Hus's preaching resonated deeply with the common people but provoked the ire of Church authorities. His call for reform, grounded in biblical authority, struck at the heart of ecclesiastical power. His growing influence in Bohemia placed him in direct conflict with the Church's leadership.

Conflict with the Church

In 1408, the Archbishop of Prague condemned Wycliffe's teachings and ordered the destruction of his writings. Hus refused to comply. As a result, he was excommunicated in 1411. Despite this, Hus continued to preach, write, and defend the right of the people to read and hear the Scriptures in their own language.

The crisis escalated when Pope John XXIII authorized the sale of indulgences to finance a crusade against a rival claimant to the papacy. Hus condemned the sale of indulgences from the pulpit, denouncing it as a blatant perversion of biblical truth and a disgrace to the Church. This act gained him even more support among the Bohemian people—but intensified the determination of Church leaders to silence him.

Prague was placed under interdict, suspending all religious services. This was a severe punishment meant to pressure the city's authorities to act against Hus. To prevent further hardship for the people, Hus voluntarily left Prague in 1412 and continued his ministry in rural Bohemia. Even in exile, his writings and sermons reached wide audiences, and his influence continued to grow.

The Council of Constance

In 1414, Holy Roman Emperor Sigismund convened the Council of Constance, primarily to resolve the Western Schism, in which multiple men claimed to be pope. The council also aimed to address the growing calls for reform, particularly those associated with Hus. Despite the danger, Hus agreed to attend the council to defend his views, having received a promise of safe conduct from Emperor Sigismund.

Upon arrival in Constance, Hus was arrested, imprisoned, and denied the opportunity to present a full defense. The promise of safe conduct was ignored. He spent months in filthy conditions, suffering from illness and isolation. Nevertheless, he remained steadfast in his faith and convictions.

At the trial, Hus refused to recant unless he could be shown from Scripture that his views were in error. The council, however, was not interested in a biblical defense. They had already condemned Wycliffe's teachings and saw Hus as a dangerous heretic. His insistence on the primacy of Scripture over the authority of the Church sealed his fate.

Martyrdom

On July 6, 1415, the Council of Constance formally declared Hus a heretic. He was stripped of his clerical garments, humiliated, and handed over to the secular authorities. He was then led to the stake to be executed by burning.

As he was tied to the post and the fire was prepared, Hus is reported to have said, "Lord Jesus, it is for you that I patiently endure this cruel death. I pray you to have mercy on my enemies." As the flames consumed his body, he sang hymns and psalms until his voice was silenced. His ashes were thrown into the Rhine River in an attempt to erase his memory—but his legacy could not be extinguished.

The Legacy of John Hus

The martyrdom of John Hus sent shockwaves through Bohemia and beyond. Rather than silence him, his death galvanized the movement for reform. His followers, known as the Hussites, continued to preach and spread his teachings, many of which were rooted in the authority and accessibility of Scripture.

The Hussite movement played a significant role in the history of Bohemia, both spiritually and politically. It challenged papal authority, rejected unscriptural traditions, and demanded that the Bible be the supreme rule of faith and practice. Though often brutally suppressed, the movement endured and prepared the way for the broader Protestant Reformation a century later.

Martin Luther himself acknowledged Hus as a predecessor. After reading Hus's writings, Luther famously said, "We are all Hussites without knowing it." The same commitment to the Scriptures that fueled Hus's ministry would become foundational to the reformers of the sixteenth century.

Faithfulness to the Text of Scripture

John Hus did not produce a full Bible translation, but he strongly supported the idea that the Scriptures should be available in the language of the people. He promoted the translation of biblical texts into Czech and worked to disseminate the Word of God among those who had been kept in ignorance by Latin-only services and preaching.

His advocacy for the authority of Scripture over ecclesiastical tradition was inseparable from his desire to see the Bible translated accurately and read by all. He recognized the grave danger of a Church that placed itself above the Word of God. His insistence that truth be derived from Scripture alone remains central to any faithful Bible translation effort.

Hus's martyrdom reminds us of the cost of fidelity to God's Word and the obligation of translators, preachers, and teachers to uphold it without compromise.

The Influence on Future Translation Efforts

Though Hus was condemned and executed, his work contributed to the larger movement that would eventually see the Scriptures translated from the original languages into many tongues. His teachings inspired others to pursue reform, and his writings continued to circulate underground.

Later reformers, particularly William Tyndale, shared Hus's belief that the Bible must be available in the language of the common people. The guiding principle in all of these efforts was that the Scriptures belong to the people of God—not to a religious elite. That vision, rooted in Hus's example, continues to shape Bible translation today.

The Hussite Movement

The Hussite movement, emerging from Hus's teachings and martyrdom, played a pivotal role in Bohemian religious history. This movement was characterized by its rejection of indulgences, clerical corruption, and the unbiblical control exerted by the Roman Church. It emphasized the authority of Scripture and demanded the administration of both the bread and the wine to all believers during communion—something the Roman Church reserved for the clergy.

The movement endured persecution, yet it achieved notable victories during the Hussite Wars, resisting both papal and imperial forces. Though it eventually fragmented, the Hussite emphasis on Scripture remained a spiritual inheritance passed to later generations of reformers.

Hus's Writings and Doctrinal Views

Among Hus's most influential works was *De Ecclesia* (On the Church), in which he argued that Christ, not the Pope, is the true head of the Church. He emphasized that the Church is composed of the elect—those who truly follow Christ—and not merely the institutional hierarchy.

In his treatise *De Simonia*, Hus condemned the widespread corruption of buying and selling church offices. He upheld the need for purity and accountability in those who claimed to shepherd the flock of God. His writings were steeped in Scripture, reflecting a deep respect for the Word and a desire to see the Church reformed in accordance with biblical teaching.

Even while imprisoned in Constance, Hus wrote letters of encouragement and instruction to his followers. These letters reveal a man whose confidence was rooted in the promises of Scripture, not in the approval of men.

The Broader Impact of His Martyrdom

Hus's death became a symbol of the high cost of opposing falsehood with truth. It demonstrated that true reform—reform grounded in Scripture—would not come easily. His execution by burning was intended to destroy both his life and his influence, but instead, it sparked greater resolve in those who remained.

The corruption and hypocrisy of the Council of Constance, so clearly on display in its treatment of Hus, discredited the Church in the eyes of many. This event, combined with growing dissatisfaction across Europe, helped to set the stage for the Reformation of the sixteenth century.

Hus's life shows that reform begins not in the halls of power but in the hearts of those who tremble at God's Word. His legacy belongs not just to Bohemia, but to every Christian who cherishes the authority of the Bible above the traditions of men.

CHAPTER 4 The Betrayal and Death of the Translator William Tyndale

William Tyndale's life and work represent a turning point in the history of Bible translation. His unwavering dedication to making the Scriptures accessible to the English-speaking world helped lay the groundwork for nearly every English Bible that followed. Tyndale was not content with paraphrases or translations from Latin. He went to the original Hebrew and Greek texts—motivated by a desire for accuracy, a reverence for Scripture, and a commitment to truth. His efforts ultimately cost him his life, but his legacy continues to shape the English Bible and the faith of countless believers.

Early Life and Education

Tyndale was born around 1494 in Gloucestershire, England. He received his education at Oxford and later studied at Cambridge, where he was introduced to the growing movement of Renaissance humanism. These academic environments prepared him linguistically and intellectually for the rigorous work of Bible translation.

He mastered several languages, including Greek, Hebrew, Latin, French, German, and Spanish. Most importantly, he became convinced that the Scriptures should be available to all people in their native tongue. At that time, the only officially sanctioned Bible was the Latin Vulgate—a version largely inaccessible to the common English speaker.

Tyndale's guiding conviction was simple and resolute: the Bible belonged to the people. Famously, he once declared to a clergyman, "If God spare my life, ere many years I will cause a boy that driveth the plough shall know more of the Scripture than thou dost." This statement captured his belief that Scripture was not the private domain of the clergy but the possession of every Christian.

Commitment to Translation

Tyndale was the first to translate large portions of the Bible into English directly from the original languages. He bypassed the Latin Vulgate entirely. His translation of the New Testament from Greek, completed in 1525 and published in 1526, was a landmark in biblical scholarship and the history of the English Bible. It was the first printed New Testament in English and the first to be mass-produced thanks to the printing press.

Tyndale adhered to a literal translation philosophy. He was committed to accurately rendering each word and phrase as it appeared in the original text. His goal was to give the English reader what the inspired authors actually wrote—not what the Church thought they meant.

This dedication to literal accuracy made his work revolutionary. It also made it dangerous. Tyndale's translation undermined the Church's control over biblical teaching and exposed many of the errors and traditions that had accumulated over centuries.

Opposition and Flight to the Continent

Tyndale's efforts to gain approval for his translation in England were quickly thwarted. The Roman Catholic Church viewed vernacular translations as heretical and subversive. Faced with opposition from religious and political authorities alike, Tyndale fled England in 1524 to continue his work in secret on the Continent.

He settled in Hamburg and later in Antwerp, both of which provided greater freedom to work and access to printing presses. During these years, he completed not only the New Testament but also translated large portions of the Old Testament directly from Hebrew—including Genesis, Exodus, Leviticus, Numbers, Deuteronomy, Joshua, Judges, Ruth, and parts of the historical books.

Despite the need for secrecy, Tyndale's work was quickly smuggled into England. His New Testaments were hidden in bales of cloth and barrels of goods, shipped into English ports, and distributed throughout the countryside. The Church reacted by hunting down these copies and burning them in public squares. But the more they burned, the more determined the people became to read the Scriptures in their own language.

Betrayal and Arrest

Tyndale's growing influence and the spread of his translations attracted attention from Church officials determined to silence him permanently. In 1535, he was betrayed by an Englishman named Henry Phillips, who had pretended to be a supporter. Phillips lured Tyndale into a trap in Antwerp, where he was seized and imprisoned in the castle of Vilvoorde near Brussels.

Tyndale was incarcerated for over a year in harsh conditions. During this time, he continued to write and translate as best he could. In one surviving letter from prison, he requested warmer clothes, a Hebrew Bible, and materials to continue his work. Even in chains, his mind and spirit remained fixed on the task of Bible translation.

Trial and Execution

Tyndale was charged with heresy and brought before ecclesiastical authorities. The accusations centered on his translation work, his rejection of unscriptural Church traditions, and his embrace of justification by faith. Though given the opportunity to recant, he refused.

On October 6, 1536, Tyndale was executed. He was first strangled, then burned at the stake. His final words are reported to have been, "Lord, open the King of England's eyes." This dying prayer would be answered in part just a few years later when King Henry VIII authorized the Great Bible—much of which was based on Tyndale's work.

THE CHALLENGE OF TRANSLATING TRUTH

Tyndale's death was the tragic climax of a life devoted to the truth of Scripture. Though his enemies tried to erase his influence, they could not silence the Word of God he had so faithfully translated.

The Legacy of William Tyndale

Tyndale's translation of the New Testament and large parts of the Old Testament became the foundation for nearly every English Bible that followed. The Matthew Bible (1537), the Great Bible (1539), the Geneva Bible (1560), and the King James Version (1611) all drew heavily from his work—some passages verbatim.

Tyndale shaped not only the religious life of English speakers but the English language itself. Phrases like "let there be light," "the powers that be," "the salt of the earth," and "the signs of the times" all entered the language through his translation. His clarity, accuracy, and elegance in rendering Scripture were unmatched.

More than any single English translator, Tyndale brought the Bible to the common man in his own tongue, and he did so with scholarly precision and theological conviction.

Tyndale's Translation Philosophy

Tyndale's approach to translation was based on reverence for the text of Scripture. He did not believe it was the translator's role to interpret what the authors might have meant. Rather, his task was to give readers what they said. Interpretation was the responsibility of the reader, guided by the context, historical setting, and study of the Word itself.

Tyndale's literal translation philosophy meant that he preserved key theological terms with consistency. He rendered the Greek word *ekklesia* as "congregation" instead of "church" to reflect its original meaning. He translated *presbuteros* as "elder" rather than "priest," challenging the Church's traditional terminology. These choices were not simply linguistic—they were theological statements meant to align the translation with the true meaning of the original text.

Impact on English Language and Faith

Tyndale's translation not only influenced doctrine but also the development of the English language. His careful selection of words, cadence, and structure helped elevate English as a literary and theological language. His Bible was readable, elegant, and powerful. It was English at its best—clear, forceful, and dignified.

Moreover, his translation provided English-speaking believers with direct access to the inspired Word of God. It shifted authority from the clergy to the Scriptures, placing the Bible in the hands of the laity. This democratization of Scripture was a monumental step in the progress of the Reformation and the spiritual awakening of the English-speaking world.

The Role of Tyndale's Supporters

Tyndale's success was not achieved in isolation. A network of supporters—merchants, reformers, and scholars—assisted him financially, provided shelter, and helped smuggle his translations into England. Humphrey Monmouth, a wealthy London merchant, offered Tyndale hospitality and funding. Others risked arrest and execution to carry and distribute his Bibles.

These supporters believed in the cause of biblical truth and saw Tyndale's translation work as vital to spiritual freedom. Without their sacrifices and loyalty, Tyndale's impact would have been severely limited.

Influence on Later Translations

Tyndale's work formed the backbone of future English Bibles. More than 80% of the King James Version's New Testament is based on Tyndale's rendering. Even many of its Old Testament passages echo his precise wording. His style and substance endured because of their quality and accuracy.

By setting the standard for biblical English, Tyndale ensured that subsequent translations retained fidelity to the original texts.

Translators who followed in his footsteps continued to prioritize literal accuracy and theological precision because he had shown what could be achieved.

Historical Context

Tyndale's work must be understood within the context of the early sixteenth century, when the Reformation was taking root across Europe. Martin Luther had translated the New Testament into German in 1522. The invention of the printing press allowed for mass production of vernacular Bibles for the first time in history.

Yet in England, the Roman Catholic Church still controlled religious life. The clergy interpreted Scripture, services were conducted in Latin, and laypeople were discouraged from reading the Bible. Tyndale defied this system by giving the people what the Church feared most: the unfiltered Word of God.

His efforts reflected the larger movement to return to Scripture as the final authority. In this sense, he was not just a translator—he was a reformer. His work opened the door for future generations to know and follow God through the Scriptures.

SECTION TWO Translation Philosophy, Process, and Differences

The debate between functional equivalence and formal equivalence in Bible translation has long been a contentious one. However, framing this debate as a dichotomy between function and form is misleading. This chapter aims to dispel the notion that translators must choose between these two approaches, advocating instead for a strict adherence to a literal translation philosophy. Our primary purpose is to present the Bible as it was given by God through His human authors, without the interference of human interpretation. Truth matters, and translating truth requires fidelity to the original text.

Understanding the False Dichotomy

The dichotomy between function and form suggests that translators must either prioritize the meaning (function) of the text or its exact wording and structure (form). This perspective implies that one must sacrifice either clarity for accuracy or accuracy for clarity. However, this is a false choice. A truly faithful translation will maintain both the form and function of the original text by adhering strictly to its words and structure, allowing the meaning to emerge naturally.

Literal translation does not disregard the function of the text. Instead, it recognizes that the form in which the Bible was written is intrinsically linked to its function. The specific words, phrases, and structures chosen by the original authors under divine inspiration carry the intended meaning. Altering these elements under the guise of clarifying function risks distorting the message.

The Pitfalls of Functional Equivalence

Functional equivalence, or dynamic equivalence, prioritizes conveying the thought or idea behind the text rather than its exact wording. This approach often leads translators to rephrase or paraphrase the original language to make it more accessible to contemporary readers. However, this method introduces several risks and challenges.

Interpretive Bias: Functional equivalence inherently involves the translator's interpretation of the text. By deciding what the original authors "meant," translators impose their understanding and potential biases on the text, which can alter the intended message.

Loss of Nuance: The specific words and structures chosen by the biblical authors were intentional and carry nuances that can be lost in a functional translation. These nuances are essential for a full understanding of the text and should not be sacrificed for the sake of readability.

Theological Implications: Functional translations can inadvertently introduce theological biases, as the translator's interpretation of a passage may reflect their doctrinal views. This can lead to translations that support specific theological positions rather than faithfully conveying the original text.

Reader Disempowerment: By interpreting the text for the reader, functional translations deprive readers of the opportunity to engage directly with the Scriptures and form their own understanding. This undermines the principle that the meaning of a word is the responsibility of the interpreter, not the translator.

The Case for Formal Equivalence

Formal equivalence, or literal translation, seeks to reproduce the exact words and structures of the original text as closely as possible. This approach respects the divine inspiration of the Scriptures and maintains the integrity of the original message. Formal equivalence provides several significant advantages:

Accuracy: By adhering closely to the original text, formal equivalence ensures that the translation remains accurate and faithful to the words chosen by the biblical authors. This accuracy is crucial for preserving the intended meaning.

Consistency: A literal translation maintains consistency in rendering key theological terms and concepts, allowing readers to trace these themes throughout the Bible. This consistency aids in a deeper understanding of the Scriptures.

Preservation of Nuance: The nuances of the original language, including wordplay, parallelism, and rhetorical devices, are preserved in a literal translation. These elements contribute to the richness and depth of the biblical text.

Reader Empowerment: By presenting the text as it was written, literal translations empower readers to engage directly with the Scriptures. This approach encourages readers to study, interpret, and apply the text for themselves, guided by the Holy Spirit.

Addressing Common Objections

Critics of formal equivalence often argue that literal translations are difficult to understand and may be less accessible to modern readers. However, these concerns can be addressed without compromising the integrity of the translation.

Clarity and Readability: While maintaining literal accuracy, translators can ensure that the translation is clear and readable by paying attention to grammar, punctuation, and syntax. Careful attention to these elements can produce a translation that is both faithful and accessible.

Footnotes and Commentary: To aid understanding, translators can provide footnotes and commentary that explain difficult passages, cultural references, and historical context. This supplementary material can enhance comprehension without altering the text.

Education and Study Aids: Promoting biblical literacy and providing study aids can help readers engage with literal translations.

Bible studies, educational programs, and resources can equip readers to understand and apply the Scriptures accurately.

The Role of the Translator

The role of the translator is to faithfully convey the original text without inserting personal interpretation. This task requires a deep understanding of the original languages, cultures, and contexts in which the Scriptures were written. Translators must approach their work with humility, recognizing that their responsibility is to preserve the integrity of God's Word.

Translators should be committed to accuracy and faithfulness, avoiding the temptation to simplify or reinterpret the text. By maintaining the original wording and structure, they ensure that the translation remains true to the inspired Scriptures. This commitment to literal translation upholds the principle that the meaning of a word is the responsibility of the interpreter, not the translator.

Conclusion

The dichotomy between function and form in Bible translation is a false one. A truly faithful translation maintains both the form and function of the original text by adhering strictly to its words and structure. Literal translation respects the divine inspiration of the Scriptures and preserves their message with the utmost accuracy.

By rejecting functional equivalence and embracing formal equivalence, translators can ensure that readers receive an accurate and faithful representation of God's Word. This approach empowers readers to engage directly with the Scriptures, guided by the Holy Spirit, and allows the meaning of the text to emerge naturally.

Edward D. Andrews

CHAPTER 5 Basics of Bible Translation

Translating the Bible is a sacred responsibility that demands accuracy, linguistic competence, and unwavering dedication to the text of Scripture. It is not merely a scholarly task but a divine commission to render God's Word faithfully from the original languages into modern vernaculars. Throughout history, Bible translation has involved both tremendous effort and significant sacrifice. This chapter explores the essential elements of the translation process, emphasizing the need for literal fidelity to the original Hebrew, Aramaic, and Greek texts.

The Original Languages of the Bible

The Bible was written in three languages: Hebrew, Aramaic, and Greek. Each presents its own unique linguistic features and challenges.

Hebrew, the primary language of the Old Testament, is a Semitic language composed of root-based words that often carry a range of related meanings. Its grammar is relatively compact, relying heavily on context to convey specific nuances. Because ancient Hebrew lacks many abstract terms and often conveys thought through concrete imagery, the translator must be well-versed in how Hebrew expressions function both grammatically and contextually.

Aramaic, a closely related Semitic language, was the common language of the Near East during much of the Old Testament and into the New Testament era. Significant portions of Daniel and Ezra, along with certain sayings of Jesus in the Gospels (e.g., *Talitha cumi*, *Eli Eli lama sabachthani*), were written in Aramaic. Although its structure is similar to Hebrew, it has distinct vocabulary and idioms.

Greek, the language of the New Testament, is an Indo-European language with a well-developed system of grammar and a precise vocabulary. Koine Greek—the common dialect of the eastern Roman Empire from roughly 300 B.C.E. to 300 C.E.—was the language of the

New Testament authors. Its grammatical precision allows for detailed expression, including case structures, verb tenses, and participles, all of which must be carefully preserved in translation to retain the meaning of the text.

The goal of Bible translation is to take these original texts and render them faithfully into the target language—accurately, clearly, and without adding or subtracting from their meaning.

The Necessity of Literal Translation

A literal translation philosophy, also known as formal equivalence, aims to preserve the exact words and sentence structures of the original language as closely as possible. This method prioritizes what the text says over what the translator thinks it means. By keeping to the words themselves and their grammatical form, literal translations allow readers to engage with the inspired text more directly.

The alternative—dynamic equivalence or thought-for-thought translation—introduces an interpretive layer that may distort the message. Translators who rely on dynamic equivalence insert their understanding into the rendering, thereby shifting the reader's focus from the inspired words to the translator's assumptions. Literal translation avoids this by preserving the text's wording and allowing meaning to emerge through careful reading, guided by context and sound interpretation.

When the original text is difficult or ambiguous, the translator's duty is not to clarify it by rephrasing or smoothing it over, but to retain the ambiguity and supply explanatory notes if necessary. This ensures that what the biblical authors wrote remains intact, and that readers, pastors, and scholars can make informed interpretive decisions.

The Translation Process

The task of translation involves several essential steps that help ensure the final product is as faithful as possible to the original Scriptures.

1. Textual Criticism

The first step is establishing the best possible form of the original text. This involves evaluating thousands of ancient manuscripts and fragments. Through textual criticism, scholars identify scribal errors, harmonizations, and interpolations, and reconstruct the wording most likely to be original.

Textual critics prioritize older manuscripts, especially those with Alexandrian characteristics. While no single manuscript contains the entire Bible, comparisons between early papyri, uncials, minuscules, and ancient versions provide a remarkably consistent witness to the original text. Textual criticism is not guesswork but an evidence-based science that provides the foundation for any translation effort.

2. Lexical and Syntactical Analysis

Once the text is established, each word and phrase must be understood in its linguistic context. This includes:

- Lexical analysis: Identifying the correct meaning of a word in its specific usage.
- Syntactical analysis: Understanding how words relate to one another in the sentence.
- Contextual analysis: Considering how the term fits within the broader passage and biblical theology.

For example, the Greek word *logos* can mean "word," "reason," "message," or "principle," depending on the context. A literal translation retains the word *logos* as "word," unless the structure demands otherwise, and explains additional nuances through footnotes if needed.

3. Rendering into the Target Language

Once the original words and grammar are understood, they must be faithfully conveyed into the target language. A literal translator seeks to preserve as much of the original sentence structure, vocabulary, and tone as possible, adjusting only when necessary for grammar or clarity.

For instance, if Hebrew parallelism or Greek participial clauses are present, the translator should maintain the structure to reflect the original rhythm or argumentation. If a term has no exact equivalent in the target language, it is retained with a footnote (e.g., *hesed* in Hebrew, or *amen* in Greek).

Literal translators do not simplify, paraphrase, or explain within the text. Interpretation belongs in notes or commentaries, not in the translation itself.

Principles Guiding Faithful Translation

Faithful Bible translation is governed by several non-negotiable principles:

Accuracy – The translation must precisely reflect the original text, preserving its meaning, grammar, and vocabulary. Every word matters, and deviations must be justified based on textual or grammatical necessity.

Consistency – Key terms must be translated the same way throughout the Bible unless context demands otherwise. Terms such as *dikaiosune* (righteousness), *agape* (love), *ekklesia* (congregation), and *pneuma* (spirit) must be rendered with consistency to preserve theological continuity.

Transparency – Literal translations do not hide difficulties. When a text is ambiguous or uncertain, the translator should provide a footnote or marginal note—never alter the text to smooth over the issue.

Faithfulness – The translator is a steward, not a commentator. The responsibility is to render what the text says, not what the translator wishes it said. Faithfulness includes resisting pressures to conform to cultural trends or theological agendas.

Clarity without Compromise – A literal translation may include updated grammar, spelling, and modern vocabulary, but never at the cost of altering the meaning or inserting interpretation. Clarity can be achieved while remaining strictly faithful.

Challenges in Bible Translation

Literal Bible translation involves many challenges, some of which are unavoidable due to the nature of language.

Idioms and Figurative Language

Every language has idioms—phrases that mean something different than their literal words suggest. In Hebrew, for example, "to uncover the feet" can be a euphemism for sexual relations. "To lift the face" means to show favor. Literal translations retain such idioms and offer explanatory notes when needed rather than substituting them with modern phrases.

Preserving idioms maintains the biblical worldview and poetic beauty of Scripture. Replacing them can destroy important theological or literary connections.

Grammatical and Structural Differences

Languages have differing syntax. Hebrew places verbs at the beginning of the sentence; Greek often uses participial chains and compound clauses. A literal translator will retain these structures as much as clarity allows. While some adjustment is necessary for the target language to make sense, the goal is minimal alteration and maximum retention of the original flow.

Vocabulary Gaps

Some biblical words have no direct equivalent in the modern language. For example:
- *Hesed* (Hebrew) conveys loyal love, mercy, and covenant faithfulness all at once.
- *Pneuma* (Greek) means spirit, breath, or wind.
- *Sheol* has no English equivalent; it denotes the common grave or realm of the dead.

Rather than replacing these with limited terms or interpretive phrases, a faithful translator retains the original concept and explains it in footnotes or a glossary.

Theological Pressure

Perhaps the greatest challenge is resisting doctrinal bias. Translators must not mold the text to support their views or their audience's expectations. Literal translation protects the text from human tampering and allows theology to emerge from Scripture, not be imposed on it.

THE CHALLENGE OF TRANSLATING TRUTH

The Role of Translation Committees

While some translations are the work of a single scholar, most modern versions are produced by committees of experts. Ideally, these teams consist of scholars skilled in Hebrew, Aramaic, and Greek; textual criticism; linguistics; and theology. Committees can check each other's work, preventing one person's bias or misunderstanding from distorting the text.

However, even committees are vulnerable to pressure—whether institutional, denominational, or commercial. When translation decisions are driven by popularity, gender politics, or modern theological trends, the result is often compromise. Faithful translators must prioritize accuracy over acceptance and integrity over innovation.

Importance of Marginal Notes and Appendices

Literal translations benefit greatly from footnotes and marginal references. These tools allow translators to provide readers with:

- Alternate manuscript readings
- Explanations of idioms
- Clarification of ambiguous words
- Background on cultural or historical references

This approach ensures transparency and allows readers to assess the data for themselves. It also protects the translation from becoming an interpretive paraphrase.

Glossaries and appendices can also help explain key terms without inserting commentary into the body of the text.

The Spiritual Responsibility of the Translator

Bible translation is not merely linguistic—it is spiritual. The translator is entrusted with the inspired Word of God. Every choice must be made in light of that weighty responsibility.

A translator must approach the text with reverence, humility, and fear of Jehovah. Every word rendered carries eternal significance. The translator is not permitted to shape the message, only to transmit it accurately. The Word of God is living and active, and it must be treated as such in translation.

CHAPTER 6 Translation Philosophy

The philosophy behind Bible translation determines whether the resulting work will be faithful to the inspired text or a reinterpretation filtered through human assumptions. Translation is not simply the mechanical act of replacing words from one language to another. It involves deep convictions about the nature of Scripture, the role of the translator, and the responsibilities of those who render the Word of God into modern languages. This chapter presents the foundation and principles of a sound translation philosophy, one rooted in faithfulness to the original text—because truth must be translated, not rephrased or reinterpreted.

Foundational Assumptions of Biblical Translation

A proper philosophy of translation begins with a high view of Scripture. The Bible is the divinely inspired Word of God—breathed out by Him through human authors using Hebrew, Aramaic, and Greek. Because the original autographs were inspired and without error, the translator's job is to preserve and convey that original wording as accurately as possible in the target language.

The translator must assume the sufficiency and clarity of the original text. The biblical authors, under divine guidance, said exactly what Jehovah intended them to say. The translator's role is not to guess what God meant, but to communicate what He said. The meaning is embedded in the words and grammar. Therefore, every effort must be made to preserve those words and that structure without inserting modern theological bias or interpretive gloss.

Literal vs. Dynamic Equivalence

Translation approaches fall into two broad categories: literal (formal equivalence) and dynamic (functional equivalence). These philosophies differ not only in method but in theological implications.

Literal translation seeks to preserve the words, grammar, and structure of the original text as closely as the target language allows. The translator endeavors to mirror the form of the source language, respecting word order, verb tenses, and syntactical structures while conveying the full semantic range of the original words.

Dynamic equivalence, on the other hand, seeks to convey the perceived meaning or intention of the text, often in ways that depart from the wording or grammar of the original. The translator determines what a passage means and rephrases it in modern terms, often simplifying or altering expressions to suit contemporary understanding.

While dynamic equivalence may seem more accessible, it poses serious risks. It inserts interpretation into the translation process, obscuring the boundary between what Scripture says and what the translator thinks it means. The result is often a paraphrase rather than a translation.

Literal translation preserves the inspired words and entrusts interpretation to the reader, teacher, or pastor. This distinction is critical. The translator must not become the expositor. Exegesis belongs to the pulpit and the commentary, not to the translation itself.

Why Literal Translation Matters

Literal translation protects the integrity of God's Word. The biblical text is not merely a source of theological ideas—it is itself the message. Every word, tense, mood, and construction matters. A shift in wording may lead to a shift in doctrine. Therefore, literal translation is the most honest, transparent, and faithful way to bring Scripture into another language.

Literal translation:

- Preserves authorial intent by maintaining the form and wording chosen by the biblical authors.
- Avoids doctrinal bias by not reinterpreting phrases to suit modern trends or theological agendas.
- Allows readers to trace themes, vocabulary, and grammatical patterns essential for study and interpretation.
- Encourages readers to engage directly with the structure and nuance of the original languages through the translation.

While a literal translation may require greater effort from the reader, it provides a more accurate foundation for study, preaching, and teaching. The Word of God deserves reverence and precision—not simplification.

Misconceptions About Literal Translation

Some claim that literal translation is too difficult to understand, overly wooden, or unsuitable for modern readers. However, these objections are misguided.

A faithful literal translation does not mean using archaic language or ignoring grammar rules of the target language. Clarity is essential—but not at the expense of fidelity. A well-executed literal translation is both accurate and readable. Sentence structures can be adapted carefully while preserving meaning and form. Vocabulary can be modernized where appropriate, so long as it does not alter the original word's intent.

Literal translation is not word-for-word in the strictest mechanical sense. It respects idiomatic usage and accommodates necessary grammatical adjustments, but it refuses to replace difficult or unfamiliar expressions with interpretive substitutes. The translator's goal is to bring the reader as close to the original as possible—not to domesticate the text to make it sound modern or relatable.

The Translator's Role and Ethical Boundaries

A translator is not a commentator. His task is not to explain, paraphrase, or reframe the Bible but to transfer it accurately into another language. To cross this boundary is to violate the very purpose of translation.

A faithful translator:

- Respects the text's structure and flow, even if it challenges modern sensibilities.
- Refrains from imposing theological systems or denominational biases onto the translation.
- Provides footnotes or marginal notes to clarify ambiguities, not interpret them.
- Seeks input from multiple textual witnesses to ensure accuracy.
- Acknowledges where the text is difficult and retains that difficulty, rather than smoothing it over.

Translation must be transparent. Readers should be able to see when a rendering is uncertain or when an alternate reading exists. The translator is a steward of God's Word and is accountable for every word he transmits.

Preserving Theological Terminology

Literal translation ensures consistency in rendering key theological terms. When terms are rendered faithfully, readers can trace their use across different books and contexts.

For example:

- *Dikaiosyne* should consistently be rendered "righteousness," not arbitrarily switched between "justice," "goodness," or "virtue."
- *Ekklesia* is best rendered "congregation" or "assembly," rather than "church," to avoid associations with later institutional structures foreign to the New Testament.

- *Pneuma* must consistently be "spirit," even if the context refers to the Holy Spirit, the human spirit, or breath.
- *Gehenna* should not be translated as "hell" in the sense of eternal torment but preserved for what it is—the Valley of Hinnom, symbolizing judgment and destruction.

When translators vary the rendering of such terms to suit theological agendas or simplify meaning, they undermine the unity and consistency of the biblical message.

Retaining the Structure and Literary Forms

The Bible is not only theological—it is literary. The structure of Hebrew poetry, the rhythm of Greek discourse, and the organization of biblical narrative all communicate meaning.

A literal translation respects these forms:

- Parallelism in Hebrew poetry is preserved by rendering both lines closely.
- Chiasms, inclusios, and other literary devices are maintained where possible.
- Wordplays and repetition are retained, even if they require explanation.
- Narrative flow is not restructured to match modern storytelling conventions.

Literal translation allows the reader to experience Scripture as it was written—not just in content but in style and structure. It protects the inspired literary forms that God used to communicate truth.

Avoiding Cultural Accommodation

A growing trend in modern translations is to accommodate Scripture to modern cultural values. This is especially evident in areas such as gender language, sexuality, and social roles. Literal translation resists this pressure by remaining anchored to the original languages and historical context.

Translators must not:

- Insert gender-inclusive language where the original does not warrant it.
- Soften terminology related to sin, judgment, or divine wrath.
- Replace patriarchal terms with neutral alternatives when the original is not neutral.
- Reword texts to align with political or social ideologies.

Such accommodations compromise the authority of Scripture and reshape it to conform to the reader. Literal translation guards against this by holding the text as supreme—not the culture or the sensitivities of the modern audience.

Translation and Interpretation: Distinct but Related

While translation and interpretation are separate functions, they are closely related. Every translator must make interpretive decisions, especially when words have multiple meanings or sentence structure is ambiguous. The key distinction is that the translator makes these decisions on the basis of grammar, syntax, and context—not theological preference or doctrinal tradition.

For example, when Paul uses the phrase *pistis Iesou Christou*, a literal translator will render it as "faith of Jesus Christ" and provide a footnote explaining that the Greek could also be understood as "faith in Jesus Christ." He does not choose based on his theology but based on what the grammar permits.

Literal translation respects the reader's role in the interpretive process. It does not dictate the meaning but presents the inspired text faithfully, allowing the Holy Spirit and sound exegesis to do the interpretive work.

Summary of the Literal Philosophy

A biblical philosophy of translation is rooted in reverence for Scripture and commitment to truth. Literal translation is not an academic preference—it is a spiritual necessity. Only by preserving the

THE CHALLENGE OF TRANSLATING TRUTH

words God gave can we honor His voice and communicate His will accurately.

This philosophy affirms:

- The inspiration and inerrancy of the original texts.
- The sufficiency and clarity of Scripture.
- The priority of what was written, not what is presumed.
- The translator's duty to transmit, not interpret.

Any departure from this approach opens the door to error, distortion, and confusion. Therefore, literal translation must remain the standard for faithful Bible versions. It is the only method that safeguards the original meaning, respects the authority of God's Word, and equips readers to engage directly with what was written by the prophets and apostles under divine inspiration.

Edward D. Andrews

CHAPTER 7 The Different Kinds of Bible Translations

Translating the Old Testament presents unique challenges and responsibilities for the faithful translator. Composed predominantly in Hebrew with some Aramaic portions, the Old Testament reflects ancient Semitic thought, culture, and linguistic structures that are often far removed from the modern reader's experience. Yet these writings are no less inspired than the New Testament. They are the foundation of divine revelation, the record of Jehovah's covenant dealings with His people, and the prophetic testimony that points to the fulfillment of His redemptive plan.

A proper translation of the Old Testament must remain anchored in a literal rendering of the text, preserving both form and meaning as they were originally written. Any deviation from this standard opens the door to interpretation, paraphrase, or ideological distortion.

The Hebrew Text: Foundation for Translation

The Old Testament was primarily written in Biblical Hebrew, a language that is concise, image-driven, and rich in layered meaning. Translators must understand that Hebrew often communicates truth through patterns, parallelisms, repetition, and wordplay. Many words are built from three-letter roots, and meanings often shift subtly depending on context.

The translator must become deeply familiar with:

- Hebrew verb stems (*qal*, *piel*, *hiphil*, *niphal*, etc.)
- Syntax and sentence order (which differs significantly from English)
- Lexical range of key terms (many Hebrew words have multiple legitimate uses)

- Nuanced uses of the definite article, conjunctions, and prepositions
- The poetic structure of Psalms, Proverbs, and Prophetic literature

While the Massoretic Text (MT) is the primary Hebrew source for translation, other textual witnesses—such as the Dead Sea Scrolls (DSS), the Samaritan Pentateuch, and early Greek translations—can assist in confirming or clarifying the text. Still, the MT remains the standard text used for translation, and variations must be treated carefully, never superseding the best attested form without compelling evidence.

The Aramaic Passages

Parts of the Old Testament are in Aramaic—primarily Daniel 2:4b–7:28 and Ezra 4:8–6:18; 7:12–26. Aramaic, while related to Hebrew, has distinct vocabulary, grammar, and structure.

Translators must ensure that the transition from Hebrew to Aramaic and back is not smoothed over or ignored. The inspired shift in language should be retained in a faithful translation. Explanatory notes can alert readers to the change in language and provide background without inserting interpretation into the body of the translation.

The Importance of Proper Names and Titles

One of the most critical aspects of Old Testament translation is the rendering of divine names and titles. Chief among these is the personal name of God, represented by the Tetragrammaton (יהוה). Faithful translators should render this as **Jehovah**, preserving the distinctiveness of God's name rather than replacing it with a title such as "the LORD."

Rendering Jehovah's name accurately reflects the text's emphasis on the covenant relationship between God and His people. It also ensures that readers can distinguish when the text refers specifically to Jehovah versus when it uses general terms like *El*, *Elohim*, or *Adonai*.

Other proper names and titles must likewise be handled with precision. Hebrew names often carry theological significance. For example:

- **Isaiah** (Yeshayahu) means "Jehovah is salvation."
- **Elijah** (Eliyahu) means "My God is Jehovah."

Literal translation preserves these elements either in transliteration or with footnotes explaining the name's meaning.

Literary Forms: Preserving Hebrew Poetry and Narrative

A major challenge in Old Testament translation is preserving the literary structure. Much of the Old Testament is written in poetry—especially the Psalms, Proverbs, and Prophets. Hebrew poetry does not rely on rhyme or meter but on parallelism, repetition, and structural balance.

Types of Hebrew parallelism include:

- **Synonymous parallelism** – The second line repeats the idea of the first in different words.
- **Antithetic parallelism** – The second line contrasts the first.
- **Synthetic parallelism** – The second line completes or develops the first thought.

A literal translation preserves these patterns. Rather than condensing or rewording lines for clarity or ease, a faithful rendering mirrors the original structure, maintaining the rhythm and flow of the Hebrew.

Similarly, Hebrew narrative often uses repetition, chiasm, and slow, deliberate pacing. These literary features should not be edited or restructured to fit modern storytelling preferences. The translator must retain what the author wrote, not what the reader may expect.

Difficult Expressions and Idioms

Hebrew contains many idioms—expressions whose meanings cannot be understood by literal translation alone. Yet a faithful translation will retain the idiom while using footnotes to explain it when necessary.

Examples include:

- "His nose burned" (Hebrew idiom for anger)
- "He lifted his eyes" (an idiom for looking or seeing)
- "To uncover one's feet" (a euphemism, sometimes for sexual relations)

These idioms should be translated as they stand, with footnotes providing clarification. Replacing them with modern idioms or paraphrases removes the cultural and theological flavor of the original.

Chronology and Dates

Literal translation must also reflect the text's chronological precision. The Old Testament often includes genealogies, age records, regnal years, and festival schedules—all of which are tied to the unfolding redemptive history.

While some translations generalize or paraphrase these sections, a literal translation preserves every number, date, and timeline exactly. Translators must be careful not to harmonize or simplify chronological data but present it as written, allowing scholars and students to study and resolve any complexities.

For instance, the date of the Exodus must reflect the literal biblical chronology (1446 B.C.E.), not a speculative or critical reconstruction. The translator is not to revise or modernize these dates but preserve them as recorded in the original text.

Theological Terms and Covenant Language

The Old Testament is rich in covenantal and theological terminology. Words like:

- **Torah** – Law, instruction, teaching
- **Berith** – Covenant
- **Tzedek** – Righteousness
- **Chesed** – Loyal love, covenant faithfulness
- **Nephesh** – Soul, life, person

Each of these must be handled with care. A literal translation will aim for one-to-one equivalence whenever context allows. When a term has no direct English counterpart (such as *chesed*), it is best retained with explanation rather than replaced with vague or insufficient synonyms like "love" or "mercy."

Consistency in rendering these terms across the Old Testament is essential for theological clarity. The goal is not to simplify but to preserve and explain.

Translating the Prophets: A Matter of Precision

The prophetic books present special challenges due to their complex language, poetic form, and eschatological themes. Prophets often used metaphor, symbols, and divine speech that must be translated without speculative interpretation.

A faithful translator will:

- Retain metaphorical language and divine imagery
- Refrain from replacing symbols with interpretations
- Preserve the structure and flow of divine oracles
- Translate word-for-word where possible, explaining only in notes

For example, Isaiah's vision of the "branch" (Hebrew: *tsemach*) is rich in messianic meaning. A literal rendering preserves the word "branch" and its prophetic connections across Scripture rather than replacing it with a theological label.

Similarly, apocalyptic language in Ezekiel and Daniel must be presented as-is, without conjecture. The translator's role is to preserve, not predict.

Retaining the Law as Written

The Torah (Genesis–Deuteronomy) contains detailed legal codes and covenant stipulations. Literal translation must maintain the specificity and formality of these laws. Translators must resist the temptation to simplify, summarize, or modernize legal texts.

- Laws must be rendered in their legal structure, not paraphrased.
- Repetitions and patterns must be preserved.
- Sacrificial, ritual, and ceremonial language must retain its terminology.
- Terminology for uncleanness, atonement, guilt, and purification must be translated consistently.

Literal translation enables readers to see the patterns and structure of the Law as Jehovah delivered it to Israel. This is essential for theological study, biblical theology, and understanding the context for later revelation.

Footnotes and Translation Transparency

Because Hebrew grammar and idiom can be unfamiliar, literal translations benefit from detailed footnotes that explain:

- Alternate translations
- Cultural or historical background
- Lexical notes
- Textual variants

These notes belong outside the main text so the reader can engage with the words of Scripture first, then consult the notes for help. This maintains the distinction between what God said and what scholars say about what He said.

Spiritual Responsibility in Translating the Old Testament

The Old Testament is not obsolete. It is the foundation of all Scripture and must be handled with reverence and precision. It testifies to God's creation, His covenant with Abraham, the Law given through Moses, the promise of a coming Messiah, and the unfolding plan of redemption.

The translator is accountable before God for the words he transmits. He must not shape the Old Testament to fit modern sensibilities or theological systems. Instead, he must preserve its form, voice, and content faithfully.

Literal translation is the only method that honors the original languages and preserves the inspired message given through the prophets. It is the only method that trusts the text to speak for itself and guards it from human alteration.

CHAPTER 8 The Making of a Worthy Translation

Creating a worthy Bible translation is a monumental task that demands a rigorous commitment to accuracy, faithfulness, and integrity. The translator's primary purpose is to convey what God said through His human authors, without interjecting personal interpretations or altering the text's original meaning. This chapter explores the meticulous process involved in producing a worthy Bible translation, highlighting the principles and methodologies that ensure the text remains true to its divine inspiration.

The Foundation: Understanding the Original Texts

The first step in creating a worthy translation is a profound understanding of the original texts. The Bible was originally written in Hebrew, Aramaic, and Greek, each with its own unique linguistic and cultural characteristics. A translator must be proficient in these languages, understanding their grammar, syntax, vocabulary, and idiomatic expressions.

Hebrew, the primary language of the Old Testament, is a Semitic language with a rich and complex structure. It is characterized by its consonantal script and a wide range of meanings for individual words. Understanding the nuances of Hebrew grammar and syntax is essential for accurately translating the Old Testament.

Aramaic, a closely related language, was the lingua franca of the Near East during the time of the Old Testament and parts of the New Testament. Portions of Daniel and Ezra, as well as certain sayings of Jesus, are written in Aramaic. Proficiency in Aramaic is necessary for translating these texts accurately.

Greek, the language of the New Testament, is an Indo-European language with a highly structured grammar and precise vocabulary. Koine Greek, the dialect of the New Testament, was the common language of the eastern Mediterranean in the first century C.E. Translating the New Testament requires a thorough understanding of Greek grammar, vocabulary, and idiomatic expressions.

Textual Criticism: Establishing the Most Accurate Text

Textual criticism is a critical component in the translation process. This discipline involves examining the various manuscripts of the Bible to determine the most accurate text. The Bible has been transmitted through thousands of manuscripts, some of which contain variations due to copying errors or intentional alterations. Textual critics analyze these manuscripts, comparing them and identifying the most reliable readings.

The goal of textual criticism is to reconstruct the original text as closely as possible. This involves examining the oldest and most reliable manuscripts, considering the historical and geographical context of the manuscripts, and assessing the internal consistency of the text. The results of textual criticism provide the foundation for the translation process, ensuring that translators are working from the most accurate text available.

Principles of Translation: Accuracy and Faithfulness

Several key principles guide the translation process, ensuring that the final product is both accurate and faithful to the original text:

1. **Literalness**: The translation should adhere as closely as possible to the original words and grammatical structures. This approach allows readers to engage directly with the Scriptures and draw their own interpretations based on a faithful rendering of the original text.

2. **Contextuality**: Translators must consider the context in which the text was written, including the historical, cultural, and linguistic context. This involves understanding the original audience and the specific circumstances that influenced the writing of the text.

3. **Clarity**: While maintaining literalness, the translation must also be clear and understandable to modern readers. This involves finding a balance between preserving the original meaning and making the text accessible to contemporary audiences.

4. **Consistency**: Translators should strive for consistency in their rendering of specific terms and phrases. This helps to maintain the coherence and integrity of the text, allowing readers to see the connections and themes within the Scriptures.

5. **Faithfulness**: Above all, the translation must remain faithful to the original text, avoiding interpretive additions or alterations. The goal is to provide a translation that accurately conveys the meaning and intent of the original authors, allowing readers to engage directly with God's Word.

The Role of Translation Committees

Translation committees play a crucial role in producing reliable Bible translations. These committees consist of scholars and experts from various fields, including biblical languages, theology, textual criticism, and cultural studies. The collaborative nature of these committees helps ensure that the translation reflects a broad consensus of scholarly opinion and mitigates individual biases.

Translation committees engage in rigorous review and revision processes, carefully examining each passage to ensure its accuracy and faithfulness to the original text. This collaborative approach is essential for producing a reliable and trustworthy translation.

Challenges in Bible Translation

Bible translation is not without its challenges. Translators must navigate several difficulties to produce an accurate and faithful translation. Some of these challenges include:

Linguistic Differences

The linguistic differences between the original languages of the Bible and modern languages can pose significant challenges for translators. Hebrew, Aramaic, and Greek have unique grammatical structures, idiomatic expressions, and cultural references that may not have direct equivalents in modern languages. Translators must find ways to convey these concepts accurately while maintaining the integrity of the original text.

Cultural and Historical Contexts

The cultural and historical contexts of the Bible are vastly different from those of modern readers. Translators must understand the specific circumstances that influenced the writing of the text and find ways to convey these contexts to contemporary audiences. This involves a deep understanding of the historical and cultural background of the Scriptures, as well as the ability to bridge the gap between ancient and modern contexts.

Theological Considerations

Translating the Bible also involves navigating theological considerations. Different theological traditions may have varying interpretations of specific passages, and translators must find ways to render the text accurately while remaining faithful to the original meaning. This requires a careful balance between preserving the theological intent of the authors and avoiding interpretive biases.

The Importance of Literal Translation Philosophy

A literal translation philosophy is essential for maintaining the integrity of the original text. This approach seeks to render the text as closely as possible to the original words and sentence structures, preserving the nuances and specific meanings intended by the authors. Literal translations allow readers to engage directly with the Scriptures, drawing their own interpretations based on a faithful rendering of the original text.

Interpretive translations, on the other hand, risk altering the intended meaning by imposing the translator's interpretation onto the text. While these translations may be easier to read and understand, they can lead to a distortion of the original message. Our primary goal as translators is to provide an accurate and faithful rendering of the

Scriptures, allowing readers to engage with God's Word as it was originally intended.

Case Study: The Updated American Standard Version (UASV)

The Updated American Standard Version (UASV), completed in 2022, exemplifies the principles of a worthy translation. The UASV adheres to a literal translation philosophy, striving for accuracy and faithfulness to the original text. The translation process involved meticulous textual criticism, linguistic analysis, and the application of translation principles to ensure that the final product was both accurate and clear.

The UASV's commitment to a literal translation philosophy is evident in its rendering of specific terms and phrases, its adherence to the original grammatical structures, and its effort to maintain consistency throughout the text. This approach allows readers to engage directly with the Scriptures and draw their own interpretations based on a faithful rendering of the original text.

The Role of Technology in Modern Bible Translation

Advancements in technology have significantly impacted the field of Bible translation. Digital tools and resources have made it easier for translators to access and analyze ancient manuscripts, conduct linguistic research, and collaborate with other scholars. These tools have also facilitated the dissemination of translations, making the Bible more accessible to people around the world.

Technology has enabled the creation of digital databases of biblical manuscripts, allowing translators to compare different texts and identify the most accurate readings. Software programs can assist with linguistic analysis, helping translators to understand the grammar, syntax, and vocabulary of the original languages. Online platforms enable translation committees to collaborate in real-time, streamlining the review and revision process.

The Future of Bible Translation

The future of Bible translation will likely continue to be shaped by advancements in technology, increased collaboration among scholars, and a commitment to maintaining the integrity of the original text. As our understanding of the original languages and cultural contexts deepens, translations will need to be updated to reflect the best available evidence.

Ongoing review and revision will be essential to ensure that translations remain accurate and faithful to the original meaning. This process involves a careful balance between preserving the text's accuracy and making it accessible to contemporary audiences.

Conclusion

The making of a worthy Bible translation is a complex and profound task that requires a rigorous commitment to accuracy, faithfulness, and integrity. A literal translation philosophy ensures that the text remains faithful to the original words and structures, allowing readers to engage directly with God's Word. This approach respects the original text's authority and inspiration, providing a more accurate basis for exegesis and theological study.

As we reflect on the principles and processes involved in creating a worthy translation, we are reminded of the sacrifices made by translators who have dedicated their lives to this sacred task. Their work ensures that the Scriptures remain accessible to all people, allowing believers to engage directly with the Word of God and draw strength, guidance, and inspiration from its truths.

SECTION THREE Translation Principles

Translators play a crucial role in preserving the integrity and accuracy of the Scriptures. Their task is not just to convert words from one language to another, but to faithfully convey the original message as intended by the divine and human authors. This chapter explores the responsibilities of translators, the challenges they face, and the principles they must adhere to in order to maintain the purity of God's Word. Our primary purpose is to give Bible readers what God said through His human authors, not what a translator thinks God meant. Truth matters, and our goal is to be accurate and faithful to the original text. The meaning of a word is the responsibility of the interpreter, not the translator.

The Responsibilities of Translators

Translators bear a significant responsibility in ensuring that the Scriptures remain true to their original form and message. This responsibility encompasses several key areas:

Fidelity to the Original Text: Translators must be committed to maintaining the exact wording and structure of the original texts. This involves a deep understanding of the source languages—Hebrew, Aramaic, and Greek—and a meticulous approach to translation.

Avoiding Interpretive Bias: Translators should resist the temptation to insert their own interpretations or theological biases into the text. Their role is to convey the words of the original authors accurately, leaving the interpretation to the reader.

Clarity and Readability: While maintaining literal accuracy, translators must also ensure that the text is clear and comprehensible. This involves careful attention to grammar, syntax, and word choice, while avoiding unnecessary simplification or alteration of the original message.

Transparency and Honesty: Transparency in translation is essential. This includes providing footnotes, marginal notes, and other supplementary materials to explain difficult or ambiguous passages, ensuring that readers are aware of any interpretive choices made in the translation process.

Challenges Faced by Translators

Translators encounter numerous challenges in their work, many of which stem from the complexity and depth of the biblical texts. Some of these challenges include:

Linguistic Differences: The differences between ancient Hebrew, Aramaic, and Greek and modern languages can make direct translation difficult. Translators must navigate these differences while preserving the original meaning and nuance.

Cultural Context: The cultural and historical contexts of the biblical texts are often vastly different from those of contemporary readers. Translators must convey these contexts without distorting the original message.

Textual Variants: The existence of multiple manuscript traditions and textual variants presents a challenge for translators. They must decide which variants to follow and how to represent them in the translation.

Theological Controversies: Translators often work within specific theological traditions, which can influence their approach to the text. Maintaining neutrality and avoiding doctrinal biases is crucial for preserving the integrity of the translation.

Principles for Faithful Translation

To address these challenges and fulfill their responsibilities, translators should adhere to several key principles:

Literal Translation Philosophy: A literal translation philosophy prioritizes word-for-word accuracy, maintaining the original wording and structure as closely as possible. This approach respects the divine inspiration of the Scriptures and ensures fidelity to the original texts.

Historical-Grammatical Method: The historical-grammatical method involves interpreting the text based on its historical context and grammatical structure. This method helps translators understand the original meaning and convey it accurately.

Transparency and Honesty: Providing supplementary materials such as footnotes, glossaries, and commentaries helps readers understand difficult passages without altering the text itself. This transparency ensures that readers are aware of any interpretive decisions made by the translators.

Commitment to Neutrality: Translators should strive to maintain neutrality, avoiding the influence of their own theological perspectives. This involves resisting the temptation to interpret or rephrase the text in a way that aligns with specific doctrinal beliefs.

Case Studies in Faithful Translation

Examining specific examples of faithful translation can illustrate how these principles are applied in practice:

Genesis 1:1: "In the beginning, God created the heavens and the earth." A literal translation preserves the simplicity and profundity of the original Hebrew, conveying the foundational truth of God's creation.

Isaiah 53:5: "But he was pierced for our transgressions; he was crushed for our iniquities; upon him was the chastisement that brought us peace, and with his wounds we are healed." This literal rendering maintains the vivid imagery and theological depth of the original Hebrew text.

John 1:1: "In the beginning was the Word, and the Word was with God, and the Word was God." A literal translation preserves the original Greek structure and the profound theological statement about the divinity of Christ.

The Ethical Responsibility of Translators

Translators have an ethical responsibility to faithfully convey the original text, respecting its theological and doctrinal content. This task requires dedication, expertise, and a commitment to preserving the integrity of God's Word.

Maintaining Fidelity: Translators must maintain fidelity to the original text, ensuring that their work accurately reflects the biblical authors' words and intent.

Avoiding Interpretation: Translators should resist the temptation to insert their interpretations into the text. Instead, they should provide a faithful rendering, allowing readers to explore the meaning themselves.

Ensuring Clarity: While maintaining literal accuracy, translators should also ensure that the text is clear and comprehensible. This involves careful attention to grammar, punctuation, and syntax, as well as providing supplementary materials to aid understanding.

The Role of Supplementary Materials

To support readers in understanding difficult passages, supplementary materials such as footnotes, glossaries, and commentaries can provide valuable context and explanations without altering the text itself.

Footnotes: Footnotes can offer explanations of difficult terms, cultural references, and historical context. For example, a note on "girding one's loins" in 1 Peter 1:13 can explain the cultural practice and its metaphorical meaning.

Glossaries: Glossaries provide definitions and explanations of key terms and concepts. This helps readers understand specific words and their significance within the biblical text.

Commentaries: Commentaries offer in-depth discussions of passages, providing theological insights, historical background, and linguistic analysis. These resources support readers in their study of the Scriptures.

The Future of Bible Translation

As we look to the future, the principles of literal translation remain essential for preserving the integrity of the Scriptures. Advances in technology and scholarship offer new opportunities for enhancing the accuracy and accessibility of biblical translations.

Digital Tools: Digital tools and resources can support the translation process by providing access to a wealth of manuscript evidence, linguistic data, and scholarly research. These tools can enhance the precision and efficiency of translation work.

Collaborative Efforts: Collaborative efforts among scholars, linguists, and theologians can ensure that translations are both accurate and comprehensive. By bringing together diverse expertise, translators can produce high-quality literal translations that respect the original texts.

Educational Resources: Promoting biblical literacy through educational resources and study programs can help readers engage with the Scriptures. By providing tools and guidance, we can empower readers to explore the meaning and significance of the biblical texts.

Conclusion

Translators play a vital role in preserving the integrity and accuracy of the Scriptures. By adhering to a literal translation philosophy and maintaining fidelity to the original texts, translators ensure that God's Word is conveyed faithfully and accurately. Our primary purpose is to give Bible readers what God said through His human authors, not what a translator thinks God meant. Truth matters, and our goal is to be accurate and faithful to the original text. By maintaining this commitment, we provide a clear and faithful representation of the Scriptures, allowing readers to engage directly with God's Word and discern its meaning through careful study and guidance from the Holy Spirit.

Edward D. Andrews

CHAPTER 9 Idioms in Bible Translation

Idioms in Bible Translation

The task of translating the Bible involves navigating a complex landscape of language, culture, and history. One of the most challenging aspects of this work is dealing with idioms—expressions that carry meaning beyond the literal definitions of their individual words. Idioms are deeply rooted in the cultural and linguistic context of the original text, making them particularly difficult to translate accurately. This chapter explores the nature of idioms in the Bible, the challenges they pose for translators, and the principles that guide the translation of these expressions while maintaining fidelity to the original text.

Understanding Idioms

An idiom is a phrase or expression that has a figurative meaning different from the literal meanings of its individual words. For example, the English idiom "kick the bucket" means "to die," but taken literally, it has no such meaning. In the context of Bible translation, idioms often reflect the cultural and historical background of the ancient Near Eastern and Greco-Roman worlds.

The Bible is replete with idiomatic expressions that convey rich, nuanced meanings. Understanding these idioms requires not only linguistic knowledge but also an awareness of the cultural and historical settings in which they were used. Translators must consider how to render these idioms in a way that conveys their intended meaning to contemporary readers.

Challenges of Translating Idioms

Translating idioms presents several challenges. First, idioms often do not have direct equivalents in the target language. A literal translation of an idiom may result in a nonsensical or misleading expression that fails to convey the original meaning. For instance, the Hebrew idiom "to lift up one's face" means "to show favor" or "to be pleased," but a literal translation would be confusing to most modern readers.

Second, idioms are deeply embedded in the cultural context of the original text. Understanding the cultural significance of an idiom is crucial for accurate translation. For example, the Hebrew idiom "a land flowing with milk and honey" (Exodus 3:8) conveys the idea of abundance and prosperity. Translators must ensure that the translated idiom communicates the same connotations to contemporary readers.

Third, some idioms are unique to the biblical text and have no parallels in other ancient literature. This uniqueness can make it difficult to determine the precise meaning of an idiom and how best to translate it.

Principles for Translating Idioms

To address these challenges, translators must adhere to several key principles when translating idioms:

Faithfulness to the Original Text: The translation must remain faithful to the original meaning and intent of the idiom. This involves understanding the idiom's figurative meaning and finding an equivalent expression in the target language that conveys the same meaning.

Clarity and Readability: While maintaining faithfulness to the original text, the translation must also be clear and understandable to modern readers. This may involve using a more familiar idiom or expression in the target language that conveys the same meaning.

Cultural Sensitivity: Translators must consider the cultural context of both the original text and the target audience. This involves understanding the cultural significance of the idiom and finding a way to convey that significance in the translation.

Consistency: Translators should strive for consistency in their rendering of idioms. This helps to maintain the coherence of the text and allows readers to recognize and understand recurring idiomatic expressions.

Examples of Idiomatic Translation

Several examples illustrate the application of these principles in the translation of biblical idioms:

"Lifting Up One's Face" (Genesis 32:20, UASV): The Hebrew idiom "to lift up one's face" means "to show favor." The Updated American Standard Version (UASV) renders this idiom as "to be pleased," which conveys the intended meaning in a way that is clear and understandable to modern readers.

"A Land Flowing with Milk and Honey" (Exodus 3:8, UASV): This idiom conveys the idea of abundance and prosperity. The UASV retains the literal translation, "a land flowing with milk and honey," while ensuring that readers understand its figurative meaning through contextual notes and explanations.

"Heart of Stone" and "Heart of Flesh" (Ezekiel 36:26, UASV): The idiom "heart of stone" signifies a hard and unresponsive heart, while "heart of flesh" signifies a soft and receptive heart. The UASV translates these idioms literally but provides notes to clarify their figurative meanings.

"Bury the Hatchet" (Modern Equivalent): While not a biblical idiom, this modern equivalent illustrates how translators can find familiar expressions in the target language that convey the same meaning as the original idiom. In a biblical context, a similar approach might involve using contemporary idiomatic expressions that capture the intended meaning of the ancient idiom.

The Role of Context in Understanding Idioms

Context plays a crucial role in understanding and translating idioms. The surrounding text often provides clues to the figurative meaning of an idiom, helping translators determine the best way to render it in the target language. For example, the idiom "to gird up one's loins" (1 Peter 1:13, UASV) means to prepare for action. The context of the passage, which speaks of mental readiness and self-discipline, helps clarify the idiom's meaning.

Translators must also consider the broader cultural and historical context in which the idiom was used. Understanding the customs, beliefs, and practices of the ancient world can shed light on the meaning of an idiom and inform its translation. For example, the idiom "to sit in sackcloth and ashes" (Job 42:6, UASV) reflects the ancient practice of expressing mourning and repentance. Translating this idiom requires an understanding of its cultural significance and finding a way to convey that significance to modern readers.

Balancing Literalness and Readability

Translators often face the challenge of balancing literalness with readability when translating idioms. A strictly literal translation may be difficult for modern readers to understand, while a more dynamic translation risks losing the original meaning. The key is to find a balance that preserves the idiom's figurative meaning while making it accessible to contemporary audiences.

For example, the Hebrew idiom "to eat the bread of idleness" (Proverbs 31:27, UASV) means to be lazy or inactive. A strictly literal translation might be confusing, so the UASV renders it as "does not eat the bread of idleness," which conveys the intended meaning clearly and accurately.

In some cases, it may be necessary to provide explanatory notes or footnotes to help readers understand the idiom's meaning. This approach allows translators to maintain a literal rendering while ensuring that readers grasp the figurative significance.

The Impact of Idioms on Translation Philosophy

The translation of idioms has significant implications for translation philosophy. A literal translation philosophy, which prioritizes adherence to the original text, must account for the figurative meanings of idioms. This requires a deep understanding of the original languages and cultures, as well as a careful approach to rendering idioms in the target language.

At the same time, a commitment to readability and clarity necessitates finding ways to make idiomatic expressions accessible to modern readers. This balance is essential for producing a translation that is both faithful to the original text and meaningful to contemporary audiences.

Balancing Readability and Accuracy

The task of translating the Bible involves a delicate balance between maintaining readability and ensuring the accuracy and integrity of the text. While literal translation philosophy emphasizes word-for-word fidelity to the original languages, it is also essential that the resulting translation be comprehensible to contemporary readers. This chapter explores strategies for achieving this balance, without compromising the principle that the translator's role is to convey what God said through His human authors, not to interpret what God might have meant. Truth matters, and our goal is to be accurate and faithful to the original text. The meaning of a word is the responsibility of the interpreter, not the translator.

The Primacy of Literal Translation

Literal translation prioritizes the exact words and structures of the original languages. This approach respects the divine inspiration of the Scriptures and ensures that the translation remains true to the original message. However, this can sometimes result in passages that are difficult or even extremely difficult to understand. In such cases, the responsibility lies with the reader to study and comprehend the text, rather than with the translator to simplify or interpret it.

For example, in 1 Peter 3:3, the phrase "Do not let your adornment be external, the braiding of hair and the wearing of gold ornaments or fine clothing" uses the Greek word *kosmos*, which is usually rendered "world." A literal translation of "world" in this context would be nonsensical, so it is rendered as "adornment" to make sense in English. In such rare cases, an interpretive rendering is necessary, but a footnote should be provided to explain the original term and its usual meaning.

Strategies for Maintaining Readability

While maintaining literal accuracy is paramount, several strategies can help ensure that the translation remains readable and comprehensible:

Careful Attention to Grammar and Syntax: Translators can ensure readability by paying careful attention to the grammar and syntax of the target language. This involves constructing sentences that are grammatically correct and flow naturally, while still adhering closely to the original text.

Supplementary Materials: Providing supplementary materials such as footnotes, glossaries, and marginal notes can help readers understand difficult passages without altering the text itself. These tools offer explanations, cultural context, and additional insights that aid comprehension.

Consistent Terminology: Using consistent terminology for key theological and doctrinal terms helps maintain clarity and coherence throughout the translation. This approach allows readers to trace themes and concepts more easily.

Clarity in Expression: While literal translations should preserve the original wording, clarity in expression can be achieved by choosing words and phrases that are understandable in contemporary language. This involves avoiding archaic or obscure terms that may confuse modern readers.

Retaining Ambiguity: In cases where the original text is ambiguous, it is essential to retain this ambiguity in the translation. This allows readers to engage with the text and explore its possible meanings, rather than having a specific interpretation imposed on them. Explanatory footnotes can offer alternative renderings and meanings.

Examples of Readability in Literal Translation

Examining specific examples can illustrate how these strategies can be applied to maintain readability without compromising accuracy:

Psalm 23:1: "Jehovah is my shepherd; I shall not want." This literal translation retains the divine name "Jehovah" and the imagery of God as a shepherd, while using simple and clear language.

Matthew 5:41: "If anyone forces you to go one mile, go with them two miles." This passage retains the original wording and cultural context, allowing readers to understand the concept of impressment during the Roman occupation.

John 1:1: "In the beginning was the Word, and the Word was with God, and the Word was God." The literal translation maintains the original Greek structure and theological significance, while being clear and comprehensible in English.

Addressing Difficult and Ambiguous Passages

Difficult and ambiguous passages are inevitable in a literal translation. Rather than simplifying these passages, translators should provide the necessary tools and resources to help readers engage with the text.

Footnotes and Marginal Notes: Footnotes and marginal notes can offer explanations of difficult terms, cultural references, and historical context. For example, a note on "girding one's loins" in 1 Peter 1:13 can explain the cultural practice and its metaphorical meaning.

Glossaries: Glossaries provide definitions and explanations of key terms and concepts. This helps readers understand specific words and their significance within the biblical text.

Commentaries: Commentaries offer in-depth discussions of passages, providing theological insights, historical background, and linguistic analysis. These resources support readers in their study of the Scriptures.

Handling Rare Interpretive Necessities

In rare instances where a literal rendering would result in nonsensical or misleading translations, an interpretive approach may be necessary. However, these instances should be clearly marked with footnotes explaining the original term and its usual meaning.

Example of *Kosmos* in 1 Peter 3:3: The phrase "Do not let your adornment be external, the braiding of hair and the wearing of gold ornaments or fine clothing" uses the Greek word *kosmos*, typically translated as "world." In this context, "adornment" is more appropriate. A footnote can explain that *kosmos* generally means "world" but here refers to external appearances.

Ambiguous Passages: Ambiguous passages should retain their ambiguity in translation. For instance, in 1 Corinthians 11:10, "For this reason, a woman ought to have a symbol of authority on her head, because of the angels," the ambiguity about "because of the angels" should be preserved. Footnotes can provide alternative interpretations and context.

Ethical Responsibility of Translators

Translators have an ethical responsibility to maintain the accuracy and integrity of the biblical text, while also ensuring that it is accessible to readers. This involves a commitment to truth, fidelity to the original text, and respect for the reader's role in interpretation.

Maintaining Fidelity: Translators must maintain fidelity to the original text, ensuring that their work accurately reflects the biblical authors' words and intent.

Avoiding Interpretation: Translators should resist the temptation to insert their interpretations into the text. Instead, they should provide a faithful rendering, allowing readers to explore the meaning themselves.

Ensuring Clarity: While maintaining literal accuracy, translators should also ensure that the text is clear and comprehensible. This involves careful attention to grammar, punctuation, and syntax, as well as providing supplementary materials to aid understanding.

Conclusion

Balancing readability and accuracy is a critical aspect of Bible translation. By adhering to a literal translation philosophy and employing strategies to maintain readability, translators can ensure that the Scriptures are faithfully conveyed without compromising their integrity.

Translating idioms in the Bible is a complex and challenging task that requires a careful balance of literalness, clarity, and cultural sensitivity. Idioms are deeply rooted in the cultural and linguistic context of the original text, making them particularly difficult to translate accurately. However, by adhering to principles of faithfulness, clarity, cultural sensitivity, and consistency, translators can render these expressions in a way that conveys their intended meaning to contemporary readers.

As we reflect on the challenges and principles of translating idioms, we are reminded of the importance of maintaining the integrity of the original text while making it accessible to modern audiences. The work of translation is a sacred task that requires a profound understanding of language, culture, and history, as well as a commitment to conveying the Word of God as it was originally intended.

CHAPTER 10 Translating the Unknown

Translating the Bible involves numerous complexities, one of the most significant being the challenge of translating the unknown. This term refers to words, phrases, cultural references, and idioms whose meanings are not immediately clear or that have no direct equivalents in the target language. This chapter delves into the strategies and principles for translating the unknown while maintaining a commitment to literal translation philosophy and ensuring the text remains accurate and faithful to the original.

Understanding the Unknown in Biblical Texts

The Bible, written in ancient Hebrew, Aramaic, and Greek, contains many elements that are unfamiliar to modern readers. These elements include obscure words, idiomatic expressions, and cultural references specific to the time and place in which the texts were written. Understanding and accurately translating these elements requires a deep knowledge of the original languages, cultures, and historical contexts.

Obscure Words and Hapax Legomena

One of the primary challenges in translating the unknown is dealing with obscure words and *hapax legomena*—words that occur only once in the entire Bible. These words can be difficult to translate because there are no other contexts within the biblical text to help determine their meanings.

For example, in Job 28:18, the Hebrew word "פנינים" (*peninim*) is often translated as "pearls," but its exact meaning is uncertain. Translators must rely on linguistic research, ancient translations, and comparative studies with other Semitic languages to determine the most likely meaning of such words.

Cultural and Historical References

The Bible is rich with cultural and historical references that may be unfamiliar to modern readers. These references can include customs, practices, geographic locations, and historical events. Accurately translating these references requires an understanding of the cultural and historical context of the biblical world.

For example, in Matthew 5:41, Jesus says, "If anyone forces you to go one mile, go with them two miles." This reference to Roman soldiers' practice of compelling civilians to carry their gear for a mile is rooted in the cultural context of Roman-occupied Judea. Translators must convey the intended meaning while providing the necessary background to help modern readers understand the reference.

Idiomatic Expressions

Idiomatic expressions pose another significant challenge in translating the unknown. These expressions often do not have direct equivalents in the target language and can be difficult to render accurately without losing their original meaning.

For example, the Hebrew idiom "אִשֵּׁה רֵיחַ נִיחֹחַ לַיהוָה" (*isheh reiach nichoach laJehovah*) is often translated as "an offering made by fire, a pleasing aroma to Jehovah" (Leviticus 1:9, UASV). The idiom conveys the idea of an acceptable and pleasing sacrifice to God, but a literal translation of "fire offering aroma" would be unclear to most readers. Translators must balance literalness with clarity to convey the intended meaning.

Principles for Translating the Unknown

To address the challenges of translating the unknown, translators must adhere to several key principles:

Thorough Research: Translators must engage in extensive linguistic and cultural research to determine the most accurate meanings of obscure words, idioms, and cultural references. This research involves studying ancient manuscripts, consulting scholarly works, and comparing other ancient languages and texts.

Contextual Understanding: Understanding the broader context of a passage is crucial for accurately translating unknown elements. This involves considering the immediate literary context, the cultural and historical background, and the overall message of the text.

Clarity and Readability: While maintaining a commitment to literal translation philosophy, translators must also ensure that the text is clear and readable for modern audiences. This may involve providing explanatory notes or footnotes to clarify the meaning of obscure words and references.

Faithfulness to the Original: Translators must strive to remain faithful to the original text, avoiding interpretive additions or alterations. The goal is to provide an accurate and faithful rendering that allows readers to engage directly with the Scriptures.

Collaborative Efforts: Translation committees play a vital role in addressing the challenges of translating the unknown. These committees bring together scholars with diverse expertise in biblical languages, textual criticism, theology, and cultural studies. Collaborative efforts help ensure that the translation reflects a broad consensus of scholarly opinion and mitigates individual biases.

Strategies for Translating Obscure Words

When dealing with obscure words and *hapax legomena*, translators can employ several strategies to determine the most likely meaning:

Comparative Linguistics: Translators can compare the obscure word with similar words in related languages, such as other Semitic languages for Hebrew words or other Indo-European languages for Greek words. This comparative approach can provide clues to the word's meaning based on its usage in related languages.

Contextual Analysis: Analyzing the context in which the obscure word appears can help determine its meaning. This involves considering the surrounding words, phrases, and the overall message of the passage. Contextual clues can often shed light on the intended meaning of an obscure word.

Ancient Translations: Consulting ancient translations, such as the Septuagint (Greek translation of the Old Testament) or the Vulgate (Latin translation of the Bible), can provide insights into how early translators understood the obscure word. While not infallible, these ancient translations offer valuable perspectives.

Lexical Studies: Lexical studies involve examining how the word is used in other ancient texts, both biblical and non-biblical. This broader linguistic context can help clarify the meaning of the word and its usage in different contexts.

Strategies for Translating Cultural and Historical References

Translating cultural and historical references requires a deep understanding of the biblical world and its customs. Several strategies can help ensure accurate translation:

Historical Research: Translators must engage in thorough historical research to understand the cultural and historical context of the biblical world. This involves studying ancient texts, archaeological findings, and historical records to gain insights into the customs and practices of the time.

Explanatory Notes: Providing explanatory notes or footnotes can help readers understand the cultural and historical references in the text. These notes offer background information that clarifies the significance of the reference and its meaning in the original context.

Contextual Translation: Translators must consider the broader context of the passage and how the cultural reference fits within that context. This involves understanding the overall message of the passage and how the cultural reference contributes to that message.

Strategies for Translating Idiomatic Expressions

Translating idiomatic expressions requires balancing literalness with clarity. Several strategies can help achieve this balance:

Equivalent Idioms: When possible, translators can use equivalent idioms in the target language that convey the same meaning as the original idiom. This approach maintains the figurative nature of the expression while making it understandable to modern readers.

Literal Translation with Explanation: In cases where there is no equivalent idiom in the target language, translators can provide a literal translation accompanied by an explanatory note. This approach preserves the original expression while ensuring that readers understand its figurative meaning.

Dynamic Equivalence: For particularly difficult idioms, translators may use a more dynamic approach to convey the intended meaning. This involves finding a contemporary expression that captures the essence of the original idiom while maintaining fidelity to the text's overall message.

Case Study: The Updated American Standard Version (UASV)

The Updated American Standard Version (UASV), completed in 2022, exemplifies the principles and strategies for translating the unknown. The UASV maintains a commitment to literal translation philosophy while addressing the challenges of obscure words, idiomatic expressions, and cultural references.

For example, in translating the Hebrew idiom "כּוֹתְנֵי עֹר" (*kotnei or*) in Genesis 3:21, the UASV renders it as "garments of skin" and provides a footnote explaining the cultural practice of making clothing from animal skins. This approach maintains the literal translation while providing readers with the necessary context to understand the idiom's significance.

Similarly, the UASV addresses obscure words by employing thorough linguistic research and consulting ancient translations. In Job

28:18, the UASV translates "פנינים" (*peninim*) as "coral" based on comparative linguistic studies and the context of the passage, which describes valuable materials.

Conclusion

Translating the unknown elements of the Bible—obscure words, idiomatic expressions, and cultural references—requires a careful balance of literalness, clarity, and cultural sensitivity. By adhering to principles of thorough research, contextual understanding, clarity, faithfulness, and collaboration, translators can render these elements accurately and faithfully.

The Updated American Standard Version (UASV) serves as a model for addressing these challenges, demonstrating how a commitment to literal translation philosophy can produce a reliable and accessible text. As we reflect on the complexities of translating the unknown, we are reminded of the importance of maintaining the integrity of the original text while making it accessible to modern readers.

CHAPTER 11 Translating Special Terms

The Bible is a rich and complex text, filled with special terms that carry deep theological, cultural, and historical significance. Translating these terms accurately and faithfully is a critical aspect of Bible translation, requiring a careful balance between literalness and readability. This chapter explores the challenges and principles involved in translating special terms, emphasizing the importance of adhering to a literal translation philosophy while ensuring the text remains clear and understandable to modern readers.

Understanding Special Terms

Special terms in the Bible include theological terms, proper names, cultural references, and unique expressions that hold significant meaning within the biblical context. These terms often have no direct equivalents in modern languages, making their translation particularly challenging. A faithful translation must convey the full depth of these terms without introducing interpretive biases or losing the original meaning.

Theological Terms

Theological terms are critical in conveying the doctrinal truths of the Bible. Terms such as "atonement," "justification," "sanctification," and "propitiation" carry specific theological meanings that are foundational to Christian doctrine. Translating these terms requires a deep understanding of their biblical usage and theological significance.

For example, the Greek term "ἱλασμός" (*hilasmos*) is often translated as "propitiation" (1 John 2:2, UASV). This term refers to the appeasement of God's wrath through the atoning sacrifice of Jesus Christ. A literal translation ensures that the full theological weight of the term is conveyed, allowing readers to grasp its significance within the context of the doctrine of atonement.

Proper Names

Proper names in the Bible, including names of people, places, and deities, are essential for understanding the historical and cultural context of the text. Translating proper names involves maintaining their phonetic and semantic integrity while making them recognizable and pronounceable for modern readers.

For instance, the Hebrew name "יְהוֹשֻׁעַ" (*Yehoshua*) is transliterated as "Joshua" in English (Joshua 1:1, UASV). This approach preserves the original sound and meaning of the name while making it accessible to English readers. Similarly, the name "Jehovah" is used to render the Tetragrammaton (יהוה, JHVH) in Old Testament verses, maintaining the sacred name's significance and continuity.

Cultural References

Cultural references in the Bible, such as customs, practices, and societal norms, provide important context for understanding the text. Translating these references accurately requires an understanding of the cultural and historical background of the biblical world.

For example, the Hebrew term "שַׁבָּת" (*Shabbat*) is translated as "Sabbath" (Exodus 20:8, UASV), referring to the seventh day of rest and worship in Jewish tradition. Translators must convey not only the literal meaning of the term but also its cultural and religious significance. Explanatory notes or footnotes can provide additional context to help modern readers understand these references.

Unique Expressions

Unique expressions in the Bible, such as idioms and metaphors, often have no direct equivalents in modern languages. Translating these expressions requires a balance between literalness and clarity, ensuring that the intended meaning is conveyed without losing the original nuance.

For example, the Hebrew idiom "עַל-כַּנְפֵי רוּחַ" (*al-kanfei ruach*) is translated as "on the wings of the wind" (Psalm 18:10, UASV). This expression conveys the idea of swift and powerful movement, and a literal translation preserves the poetic imagery while making it understandable to modern readers.

Principles for Translating Special Terms

To address the challenges of translating special terms, translators must adhere to several key principles:

Literalness: The translation should adhere as closely as possible to the original words and meanings of special terms. This approach ensures that the full theological, cultural, and historical significance of the terms is preserved.

Contextual Understanding: Translators must consider the broader context of the passage and the specific cultural and historical background of the terms. This involves understanding how the terms were used in their original context and conveying that meaning to modern readers.

Clarity and Readability: While maintaining literalness, the translation must also be clear and readable for modern audiences. This may involve providing explanatory notes or footnotes to clarify the meaning of special terms and cultural references.

Faithfulness to the Original: Above all, translators must remain faithful to the original text, avoiding interpretive additions or alterations. The goal is to provide an accurate and faithful rendering that allows readers to engage directly with the Scriptures.

Consistency: Translators should strive for consistency in their rendering of special terms. This helps to maintain the coherence of the text and allows readers to recognize and understand recurring terms and concepts.

Examples of Translating Special Terms

Several examples illustrate the application of these principles in the translation of special terms:

Atonement: The Hebrew term "כִּפֻּרִים" (*kippurim*) is translated as "atonement" (Leviticus 16:34, UASV), referring to the act of making amends for sin. This term carries significant theological weight, and a literal translation ensures that its full meaning is conveyed.

Justification: The Greek term "δικαίωσις" (*dikaiosis*) is translated as "justification" (Romans 4:25, UASV), referring to the declaration of righteousness by God. This term is foundational to the doctrine of salvation, and a literal translation preserves its theological significance.

Sanctification: The Greek term "ἁγιασμός" (*hagiasmos*) is translated as "sanctification" (1 Thessalonians 4:3, UASV), referring to the process of being made holy. This term is crucial for understanding the believer's growth in holiness, and a literal translation ensures its meaning is accurately conveyed.

Propitiation: The Greek term "ἱλασμός" (*hilasmos*) is translated as "propitiation" (1 John 2:2, UASV), referring to the appeasement of God's wrath through the atoning sacrifice of Jesus Christ. A literal translation maintains the theological depth of this term.

Shabbat: The Hebrew term "שַׁבָּת" (*Shabbat*) is translated as "Sabbath" (Exodus 20:8, UASV), preserving the term's cultural and religious significance while making it accessible to modern readers.

Challenges and Solutions

Translating special terms is not without its challenges. Translators must navigate linguistic differences, cultural gaps, and theological nuances to produce an accurate and faithful translation. Several strategies can help address these challenges:

Thorough Research: Translators must engage in extensive research to understand the linguistic, cultural, and theological background of special terms. This involves studying ancient texts, consulting scholarly works, and comparing other ancient languages and texts.

Collaborative Efforts: Translation committees play a vital role in addressing the challenges of translating special terms. These committees bring together scholars with diverse expertise, ensuring that the translation reflects a broad consensus of scholarly opinion.

Explanatory Notes: Providing explanatory notes or footnotes can help readers understand the meaning and significance of special terms. These notes offer additional context and clarification, enhancing the readability and accessibility of the text.

Consistent Terminology: Maintaining consistent terminology throughout the translation helps to ensure clarity and coherence. Readers can recognize and understand recurring terms and concepts, enhancing their engagement with the text.

Case Study: The Updated American Standard Version (UASV)

The Updated American Standard Version (UASV), completed in 2022, exemplifies the principles and strategies for translating special terms. The UASV maintains a commitment to literal translation philosophy while addressing the challenges of theological terms, proper names, cultural references, and unique expressions.

For example, the UASV consistently translates the Greek term "δικαιοσύνη" (*dikaiosyne*) as "righteousness" (Romans 1:17), preserving its theological significance. Similarly, the Hebrew term "יְהוָה" (Jehovah) is rendered as "Jehovah" in Old Testament verses, maintaining the sacred name's integrity and continuity.

The UASV also provides explanatory notes for cultural references and unique expressions. For instance, the Hebrew term "כַּפֹּרֶת" (*kapporet*) is translated as "mercy seat" (Exodus 25:17), with a footnote explaining its significance as the cover of the Ark of the Covenant and its role in the Day of Atonement rituals.

Conclusion

Translating special terms in the Bible requires a careful balance of literalness, clarity, and cultural sensitivity. By adhering to principles of thorough research, contextual understanding, clarity, faithfulness, and collaboration, translators can render these terms accurately and faithfully. The Updated American Standard Version (UASV) serves as a model for addressing these challenges, demonstrating how a commitment to literal translation philosophy can produce a reliable and accessible text.

As we reflect on the complexities of translating special terms, we are reminded of the importance of maintaining the integrity of the original text while making it accessible to modern readers. The work of translation is a sacred task that requires a profound understanding of language, culture, and theology, as well as a commitment to conveying the Word of God as it was originally intended.

CHAPTER 12 Translating Things that Get in the Way of Understanding

The task of translating the Bible is fraught with numerous challenges, many of which stem from elements in the original text that can hinder modern readers' understanding. These obstacles can include archaic language, idiomatic expressions, cultural references, and complex theological terms. This chapter explores how translators can address these issues while adhering to a literal translation philosophy, ensuring that the translation remains faithful to the original text and clear to contemporary readers.

Archaic Language

One of the most significant barriers to understanding is archaic language. Words and phrases that were common in past centuries can be obscure or completely unfamiliar to modern readers. While some translations, such as the King James Version (KJV), have historical and literary value, their archaic language can impede comprehension.

To address this, translators should update archaic terms with contemporary equivalents that convey the same meaning. For example, the KJV's "thou" and "thee" should be replaced with "you," and "hath" with "has." However, care must be taken to preserve the original tone and nuance of the text. The goal is to make the text accessible without diluting its meaning.

Idiomatic Expressions

Idiomatic expressions, which carry meanings that differ from the literal definitions of their individual words, pose another challenge. These expressions often do not translate directly into other languages and can confuse readers if rendered literally.

For example, the Hebrew idiom "to cover one's feet" means "to relieve oneself" (Judges 3:24, UASV). A literal translation would be misleading, so the idiom should be translated to convey its intended meaning clearly and accurately. In this case, "relieving oneself" would be an appropriate translation. Explanatory footnotes can also be used to provide additional context and clarify idiomatic expressions.

Cultural References

Cultural references in the Bible can be difficult for modern readers to understand. These references include customs, practices, and societal norms that were familiar to the original audience but are foreign to contemporary readers.

For instance, the practice of "gleaning" in the fields (Leviticus 19:9–10, UASV) was a well-known agricultural practice in ancient Israel, allowing the poor to collect leftover crops. Modern readers may not be familiar with this practice, so translators should provide explanatory notes or footnotes to explain the cultural context. This helps readers understand the significance of such references and their relevance to the biblical message.

Complex Theological Terms

The Bible contains numerous complex theological terms that carry deep doctrinal significance. Terms like "justification," "sanctification," "atonement," and "propitiation" are foundational to Christian theology and must be translated with precision.

For example, the Greek term "δικαίωσις" (*dikaiosis*) is translated as "justification" (Romans 4:25, UASV). This term refers to the act of being declared righteous by God, a key concept in Pauline theology. A literal translation is essential to convey its full theological meaning. However, providing additional explanatory notes can help readers grasp the term's significance within its theological context.

THE CHALLENGE OF TRANSLATING TRUTH

Strategies for Overcoming Barriers to Understanding

To effectively address the elements that get in the way of understanding, translators must employ several strategies:

Update Archaic Language: Replace archaic terms with contemporary equivalents while preserving the original tone and nuance. This ensures that the text is accessible to modern readers without losing its meaning.

Clarify Idiomatic Expressions: Translate idiomatic expressions in a way that conveys their intended meaning clearly. Use explanatory footnotes to provide additional context when necessary.

Explain Cultural References: Provide explanatory notes or footnotes to clarify cultural references and practices that may be unfamiliar to modern readers. This helps readers understand the significance of these references within their historical and cultural context.

Maintain Theological Precision: Translate complex theological terms literally to preserve their doctrinal significance. Provide additional explanatory notes to help readers understand these terms within their theological context.

Collaborative Efforts: Translation committees, consisting of scholars with diverse expertise in biblical languages, theology, and cultural studies, play a crucial role in ensuring that the translation is accurate and accessible. Collaborative efforts help mitigate individual biases and ensure a well-rounded translation.

Case Study: The Updated American Standard Version (UASV)

The Updated American Standard Version (UASV), completed in 2022, exemplifies the principles and strategies for addressing elements that hinder understanding. The UASV maintains a commitment to literal translation philosophy while updating archaic language, clarifying idiomatic expressions, and providing explanatory notes for cultural references and complex theological terms.

For example, in translating the Hebrew term "חֶסֶד" (*chesed*), which is often rendered as "lovingkindness" or "steadfast love," the UASV provides a literal translation while offering explanatory notes to help readers understand its rich theological and covenantal significance. Similarly, the Greek term "δικαιοσύνη" (*dikaiosyne*) is translated as "righteousness" (Romans 1:17, UASV), with additional notes explaining its theological implications.

The UASV also addresses idiomatic expressions by translating them in a way that conveys their intended meaning clearly. For instance, the idiom "to gird up one's loins" (1 Peter 1:13, UASV) is translated in a way that communicates the idea of preparing for action, with a footnote providing additional cultural context.

Conclusion

Translating elements that get in the way of understanding is a complex and nuanced task that requires a careful balance of literalness, clarity, and cultural sensitivity. By updating archaic language, clarifying idiomatic expressions, explaining cultural references, and maintaining theological precision, translators can produce a text that is both faithful to the original and accessible to modern readers.

The Updated American Standard Version (UASV) serves as a model for addressing these challenges, demonstrating how a commitment to literal translation philosophy can produce a reliable and understandable text. As we reflect on the principles and strategies for overcoming barriers to understanding, we are reminded of the importance of maintaining the integrity of the original text while making it accessible to contemporary audiences.

SECTION FOUR Translation Choices that Are Not Easy to Make

While Bible translators are no longer hung or burned at the stake, there remains significant pressure on their lives. Translators who do not align with certain groups can face severe professional ostracism, potentially impacting their ability to work. They are subject to both private and public mockery. For instance, literal translators are often unfairly depicted as outdated traditionalists, clinging to an antiquated method of translating the Word of God—standing in contrast to more modern dynamic equivalent or interpretive translators. These latter approaches are favored by many contemporary scholars and members of the Christian community who advocate for a translation method that prioritizes thought-for-thought rather than word-for-word accuracy.

Literal translators, dedicated to maintaining fidelity to the original text, face significant challenges. They are often treated with contempt, scorn, mockery, and even outright hostility. This disdain stems from a misunderstanding of their mission: to provide a translation that reflects as closely as possible the original manuscripts' intent and language. The literal approach emphasizes the importance of each word and its placement, believing that every detail in Scripture is significant and divinely inspired.

The dynamic equivalent method, on the other hand, prioritizes conveying the thought or meaning behind the text, sometimes at the expense of the precise wording. Proponents of this method argue that it makes the Bible more accessible and understandable to modern readers. However, this approach can introduce interpretive elements that reflect the translators' perspectives rather than the original authors' intent. This is a point of contention for literal translators, who argue that interpretive translations can lead to doctrinal inaccuracies and a departure from the true message of the Scriptures.

The debate between these two translation philosophies is not merely academic but has practical implications for the faith and understanding of millions of believers. Literal translators are often seen as resisting progress, yet their commitment to accuracy ensures that the foundational truths of Christianity are preserved. They argue that God's Word should be transmitted as it was given—without modern reinterpretations that could dilute or alter its meaning.

Translators dedicated to a literal approach often face significant professional and personal challenges. Their work is scrutinized more intensely, and their refusal to compromise on accuracy can lead to exclusion from mainstream academic and religious circles. This professional isolation is compounded by the ridicule they face from those who view their methods as outdated.

Despite these challenges, literal translators remain steadfast in their mission. They believe that fidelity to the original text is paramount and that any translation that strays too far from the original wording risks misrepresenting God's message. This conviction drives them to endure scorn and isolation, knowing that their work preserves the integrity of the Scriptures for future generations.

In modern times, the pressures on Bible translators have evolved, but the stakes remain high. The decision of how to translate the Scriptures is not taken lightly, as it directly affects how the Bible is understood and applied by believers worldwide. Literal translators' commitment to accuracy, even in the face of significant opposition, ensures that the Bible remains a true and reliable reflection of God's Word.

These pressures highlight the importance of supporting and understanding the work of literal translators. Their dedication to preserving the original text's accuracy is crucial in maintaining the Bible's integrity. While dynamic equivalence may offer a more accessible version of the Scriptures, it is the literal translations that provide a reliable foundation for faith and doctrine. In this ongoing debate, it is essential to recognize and respect the contributions of those who prioritize accuracy and faithfulness to the original text, ensuring that God's Word is conveyed as intended—without dilution or distortion.

THE CHALLENGE OF TRANSLATING TRUTH

In conclusion, the work of a Bible translator is fraught with challenges and pressures, but the dedication to preserving the accuracy and integrity of the Scriptures is a noble and vital task. Literal translators play a crucial role in ensuring that God's Word remains unaltered and faithful to the original manuscripts, providing a reliable foundation for believers worldwide. Their commitment, despite facing mockery and isolation, highlights the importance of upholding the true message of the Bible in a world that increasingly values convenience over accuracy.

Edward D. Andrews

CHAPTER 13 Gender-Inclusive Language in Bible Translation

The issue of gender-inclusive language in Bible translation has generated significant debate among scholars, translators, and readers. The primary concern is whether and how to adjust traditional masculine terms to reflect a more inclusive understanding without compromising the integrity and accuracy of the original text. This chapter examines the complexities and implications of using gender-inclusive language in Bible translation, emphasizing the importance of a literal translation philosophy that remains true to the original manuscripts.

Understanding Gender-Inclusive Language

Gender-inclusive language seeks to avoid the use of gender-specific terms when the intended meaning is not exclusively male. In English, this often involves replacing terms like "man" or "brothers" with gender-neutral alternatives such as "humanity" or "brothers and sisters." While well-intentioned, this approach can introduce interpretive biases and alter the original meaning of the biblical text.

The Biblical Context of Gender Language

The Bible was written in a historical and cultural context where male-centric language was common. Hebrew, Aramaic, and Greek—the original languages of the Bible—often use masculine terms to refer to groups that include both men and women. For instance, the Greek word "ἀδελφοί" (*adelphoi*) can mean "brothers" but often refers to both "brothers and sisters" depending on the context.

A literal translation philosophy respects this historical context and aims to preserve the original wording as closely as possible. This approach ensures that readers engage directly with the text as it was written, without the translator's interpretive influence.

Challenges of Gender-Inclusive Translation

Translating gender-inclusive language presents several challenges:

Accuracy and Faithfulness: Translators must balance the desire for inclusivity with the need to remain accurate and faithful to the original text. Altering gender-specific terms can introduce interpretive biases and potentially distort the text's meaning.

Clarity and Readability: Gender-inclusive language can sometimes complicate the text, making it less clear and more difficult to read. Translators must ensure that the text remains understandable while preserving its original meaning.

Theological Implications: Changes in gender language can have significant theological implications. For example, the use of "Father" to refer to God carries specific connotations that are integral to the text's meaning. Translators must consider these implications when deciding whether to use gender-inclusive language.

Principles for Gender Language in Translation

Several principles guide the approach to gender language in Bible translation:

Literalness: Adhere to a literal translation philosophy that preserves the original wording as closely as possible. This ensures that readers engage with the text in its most authentic form.

Contextual Understanding: Consider the broader context of each passage. While some terms may have a gender-specific meaning, others may be intended to include both men and women. Translators must use contextual clues to determine the most accurate rendering.

Clarity and Readability: Ensure that the translation remains clear and readable. Gender-inclusive language should not obscure the text or make it more difficult to understand.

Theological Integrity: Preserve the theological implications of gender-specific language. Terms that carry significant theological weight should be translated faithfully to maintain their doctrinal significance.

Examples of Gender Language Translation

Several examples illustrate the application of these principles in Bible translation:

"Man" and "Humanity": The Hebrew word "אָדָם" (*adam*) can mean both "man" and "humanity." In Genesis 1:26–27, *adam* is often translated as "man" to reflect both the individual and collective sense of humanity. The UASV renders this as "man" with a footnote explaining the broader meaning.

"Brothers" and "Brothers and Sisters": The Greek word "ἀδελφοί" (*adelphoi*) is often used to refer to both "brothers" and "sisters" in a communal sense. In Romans 12:1, the UASV translates *adelphoi* as "brothers," with a footnote indicating that the term can include both genders.

God as Father: The term "Father" (πατήρ, *pater*) is a significant theological term used to describe God. It carries specific connotations of authority, care, and relationship. Translating "Father" as "Parent" would dilute its theological meaning. The UASV retains "Father" to preserve the original intent and doctrinal significance.

Addressing Gender-Specific Passages

Certain passages in the Bible are explicitly gender-specific and should be translated accordingly. For instance, instructions given specifically to men or women—such as those in Ephesians 5:22–33 regarding husbands and wives—must be translated literally to maintain the text's integrity and intended meaning.

However, passages that use gender-specific language to refer to broader groups require careful consideration. In some cases, a footnote or explanatory note can clarify the inclusive intent without altering the text itself. This approach maintains the literal translation while providing additional context for the reader.

The Role of Translation Committees

Translation committees play a crucial role in addressing the complexities of gender-inclusive language. These committees bring together scholars with diverse expertise in biblical languages, theology, and cultural studies. Collaborative efforts help ensure that the translation is both accurate and faithful while considering the implications of gender-inclusive language.

Committees engage in rigorous review and discussion to determine the most appropriate rendering of gender-specific terms. This collaborative approach helps mitigate individual biases and ensures a balanced and well-considered translation.

The Impact of Modern Sensitivities

Modern sensitivities regarding gender language have influenced some contemporary translations to adopt gender-inclusive approaches. While these efforts aim to reflect contemporary understanding and promote inclusivity, they risk departing from the original text's intent and meaning.

As conservative evangelical scholars, it is essential to prioritize the accuracy and faithfulness of the translation above modern sensibilities. The goal is to convey what God said through His human authors, not to adapt the text to fit contemporary cultural norms.

Case Study: The Updated American Standard Version (UASV)

The Updated American Standard Version (UASV), completed in 2022, exemplifies a commitment to literal translation philosophy while addressing the challenges of gender-inclusive language. The UASV retains gender-specific terms where they are integral to the text's meaning and provides explanatory notes where appropriate to clarify inclusive intent.

For example, in translating Romans 1:7, the UASV uses "beloved of God" and provides a footnote indicating that the term includes both men and women. This approach maintains the literal translation while offering additional context to the reader.

In passages where gender-specific terms are theologically significant, such as references to God as "Father," the UASV retains the original wording to preserve its doctrinal integrity. This ensures that the translation remains faithful to the text's intended meaning and theological implications.

Conclusion

Translating gender-inclusive language in the Bible requires a careful balance of literalness, clarity, and theological integrity. By adhering to principles of contextual understanding, clarity, and faithfulness, translators can address the challenges of gender language while preserving the original text's meaning and intent.

The Updated American Standard Version (UASV) serves as a model for addressing these challenges, demonstrating how a commitment to literal translation philosophy can produce a reliable and accessible text. As we reflect on the complexities of gender-inclusive language, we are reminded of the importance of maintaining the integrity of the original text while making it accessible to contemporary readers.

CHAPTER 14 John 8:58 Why Should the Bible Translator Be Faithful So as to Give the Reader What God Said

John 8:58 stands as a pivotal verse in the New Testament, encapsulating a profound declaration of Jesus' identity and divinity. This verse reads: "Jesus said to them, 'Truly, truly, I say to you, before Abraham was, I am'" (UASV). This statement not only affirms Jesus' preexistence but also directly links Him to Jehovah, the God of Israel, as revealed in Exodus 3:14. The translation of this verse, therefore, demands utmost accuracy to preserve its theological depth and significance.

Context and Importance of John 8:58

To fully grasp the gravity of John 8:58, one must consider its context within the Gospel of John. This verse is part of a broader dialogue where Jesus confronts the Jewish religious leaders, challenging their understanding of lineage, faith, and true discipleship. When Jesus declares, "Before Abraham was, I am," He makes a direct claim to eternal existence and divinity, echoing Jehovah's self-identification to Moses in the burning bush: "I am who I am" (Exodus 3:14, UASV).

The Greek phrase "ἐγώ εἰμι" (ego eimi), translated as "I am," is not merely a statement of existence; it is a profound theological assertion that Jesus shares in the eternal nature of Jehovah. This declaration was so significant that it elicited an immediate reaction from His audience, who understood it as a claim to deity, leading them to attempt to stone Him for blasphemy.

Challenges in Translating John 8:58

Translating John 8:58 involves several challenges:

Theological Precision: The phrase "I am" is laden with theological meaning, directly connecting Jesus with the divine name revealed in the Old Testament. Any deviation from this wording risks diminishing its theological impact.

Grammatical Structure: The Greek construction "ἐγώ εἰμι" is straightforward yet profound. A literal translation is necessary to convey the weight of Jesus' statement.

Consistency with Scripture: The translation must be consistent with other scriptural references to Jehovah's self-identification to maintain theological coherence.

Principles for Faithful Translation

To navigate these challenges, translators should adhere to the following principles:

Literalness: A literal translation of "ἐγώ εἰμι" as "I am" is crucial to preserving the original meaning and theological significance.

Contextual Understanding: Translators must consider the broader context of the Gospel of John, understanding how Jesus' declaration fits within His dialogue with the religious leaders and the overall narrative of His ministry.

Theological Integrity: Maintaining the theological implications of Jesus' statement is paramount. This includes His preexistence, divinity, and identification with Jehovah.

Examples of Faithful Translation

The Updated American Standard Version (UASV) exemplifies these principles by rendering "ἐγώ εἰμι" as "I am," thereby preserving the literal meaning and theological depth of Jesus' words. Other translations that adhere to this principle include the New American

Standard Bible (NASB) and the English Standard Version (ESV), both of which translate the phrase as "I am."

These translations demonstrate a commitment to accuracy and faithfulness, ensuring that readers encounter the text as it was intended, without interpretive alterations that could obscure its meaning.

The Translator's Role

The role of the translator is to convey the original text's meaning accurately, without imposing personal interpretations or biases. This responsibility is especially critical in passages like John 8:58, where the theological implications are profound. Translators must approach their work with a deep sense of reverence and diligence, recognizing the sacred duty of faithfully transmitting God's Word.

Importance of Faithful Translation

Faithful translation is vital for several reasons:

Preserving Theological Truth: Accurate translation ensures that the theological truths of the Bible are maintained. In the case of John 8:58, this means clearly conveying Jesus' claim to divinity and preexistence.

Maintaining Scriptural Integrity: Faithful translation maintains the integrity of the Scriptures, allowing readers to engage with the text as it was originally written. This is essential for proper exegesis and theological study.

Facilitating Understanding: While accuracy is paramount, faithful translation also considers readability and clarity. A well-translated text allows readers to understand and apply its teachings more effectively.

Case Study: The UASV and John 8:58

The Updated American Standard Version (UASV), completed in 2022, provides an exemplary model of faithful translation in its rendering of John 8:58. By translating "ἐγώ εἰμι" as "I am," the UASV maintains the exact wording and theological implications of the original Greek text.

John 8:58

⁵⁸ Jesus said to them, "Truly, truly, I say to you, before Abraham was born, I am."[1]

This translation aligns with the Old Testament reference in Exodus 3:14, preserving the connection between Jesus and Jehovah. The UASV's commitment to accuracy and faithfulness ensures that readers can engage directly with the text and its profound theological implications.

Exodus 3:14

¹⁴ God said to Moses, "I am what I am"[2] And he said, "Say this to the sons of Israel: 'I am sent me to you.'"

Conclusion

The translation of John 8:58 exemplifies the critical importance of faithful translation. This passage's profound theological implications require a meticulous and accurate rendering that preserves the original meaning and significance. Translators must adhere to principles of literalness, contextual understanding, and theological integrity to ensure that the text remains faithful to the original.

The Updated American Standard Version (UASV) serves as a model for faithful translation, demonstrating how a commitment to accuracy and faithfulness can produce a reliable and accessible text. As we reflect on the challenges and principles of translating John 8:58, we are reminded of the sacred duty of translators to convey God's Word faithfully, allowing readers to engage directly with the Scriptures and their transformative power.

---

[1] The Greek (ἐγώ εἰμι egō eimi) is "I am." However, based on grammar and context, an alternative reading could be, "Jesus said to them, 'Truly, truly, I say to you, before Abraham came to be, I have been in existence.'"

[2] Or, based on grammar and context, an alternative reading could be, *I will be what I will be*.

CHAPTER 15 Acts 20:28 To What and to Whom Should a Good Bible Translation Be Faithful?

Acts 20:28 presents a critical verse in understanding the responsibilities and fidelity of Bible translation. In this passage, the apostle Paul exhorts the Ephesian elders, saying, "Pay careful attention to yourselves and to all the flock, in which the Holy Spirit has made you overseers, to care for the church of God, which he obtained with his own blood" (UASV). This verse underscores the importance of faithfulness in both doctrine and practice, serving as a guiding principle for Bible translators.

The Context and Importance of Acts 20:28

Acts 20:28 is part of Paul's farewell address to the Ephesian elders at Miletus. His words are laden with pastoral concern and theological depth, emphasizing the grave responsibility entrusted to church leaders. This verse encapsulates key themes such as the role of the Holy Spirit, the sacrificial nature of Christ's atonement, and the stewardship of God's church. Translators must approach this verse with a commitment to accuracy and faithfulness, ensuring that its theological and pastoral significance is preserved.

Challenges in Translating Acts 20:28

Translating Acts 20:28 involves several challenges:

1. **Theological Precision:** The phrase "which he obtained with his own blood" is a powerful declaration of the sacrificial atonement of Christ. Any deviation from this wording risks undermining its theological impact.

2. **Grammatical Structure:** The Greek construction, especially the genitive phrase "διὰ τοῦ ἰδίου αἵματος" (dia tou idiou haimatos), must be carefully rendered to maintain its meaning and significance.
3. **Consistency with Scripture:** The translation should align with other biblical references to the atonement and the role of church leadership, maintaining theological coherence.

Principles for Faithful Translation

To address these challenges, translators should adhere to the following principles:

1. **Literalness:** A literal translation of key phrases such as "with his own blood" is essential to preserve the theological significance of the atonement.
2. **Contextual Understanding:** Translators must consider the broader context of Paul's farewell address, understanding how this verse fits within his overall message to the Ephesian elders.
3. **Theological Integrity:** Maintaining the theological implications of Paul's statement is paramount. This includes the understanding of Christ's sacrificial death and the role of the Holy Spirit in appointing church overseers.

Examples of Faithful Translation

The Updated American Standard Version (UASV) exemplifies these principles by rendering "διὰ τοῦ ἰδίου αἵματος" as "with the blood of his own Son,"[3] thereby preserving the literal meaning and theological depth of Paul's words. Other translations, such as the New American Standard Bible (NASB) and the English Standard Version (ESV), also adhere to a literal translation philosophy in rendering this phrase accurately.

---

[3] Lit *with the blood of his Own*. Or, *with his own blood*.

These translations demonstrate a commitment to accuracy and faithfulness, ensuring that readers encounter the text as it was intended, without interpretive alterations that could obscure its meaning.

The Translator's Role

The role of the translator is to convey the original text's meaning accurately, without imposing personal interpretations or biases. This responsibility is especially critical in passages like Acts 20:28, where the theological implications are profound. Translators must approach their work with a deep sense of reverence and diligence, recognizing the sacred duty of faithfully transmitting God's Word.

The Importance of Faithful Translation

Faithful translation is vital for several reasons:

1. **Preserving Theological Truth:** Accurate translation ensures that the theological truths of the Bible are maintained. In the case of Acts 20:28, this means clearly conveying the sacrificial nature of Christ's atonement and the role of church leadership.

2. **Maintaining Scriptural Integrity:** Faithful translation maintains the integrity of the Scriptures, allowing readers to engage with the text as it was originally written. This is essential for proper exegesis and theological study.

3. **Facilitating Understanding:** While accuracy is paramount, faithful translation also considers readability and clarity. A well-translated text allows readers to understand and apply its teachings more effectively.

To What Should a Good Bible Translation Be Faithful?

A good Bible translation should be faithful to several key elements:

1. **The Original Manuscripts:** The primary objective of a good translation is to accurately reflect the original Hebrew, Aramaic, and Greek manuscripts. This involves a meticulous

examination of the textual variants and the selection of the most reliable readings.

2. **Literal Translation Philosophy:** A commitment to a literal translation philosophy ensures that the words and phrases of the original text are preserved as closely as possible. This allows readers to engage directly with the inspired Scriptures.

3. **Theological Coherence:** A good translation maintains the theological coherence of the Bible. This involves ensuring that key doctrines are accurately conveyed and that the translation aligns with the overall message of Scripture.

Whom Should a Good Bible Translation Serve?

A good Bible translation should serve several key audiences:

1. **The Faithful Reader:** The primary audience for any Bible translation is the faithful reader who seeks to understand and apply God's Word. The translation should be accessible and readable while maintaining accuracy and faithfulness.

2. **The Scholar:** Scholars rely on accurate translations for exegesis, theological study, and teaching. A good translation provides the necessary tools for rigorous academic study without interpretive biases.

3. **The Church:** The church as a whole benefits from a faithful translation that preserves the integrity of the Scriptures. This allows for sound teaching, preaching, and discipleship based on the accurate transmission of God's Word.

Challenges and Solutions in Faithful Translation

Translating passages like Acts 20:28 requires navigating several challenges. One common challenge is the temptation to paraphrase or interpret the text to make it more accessible to modern readers. While readability is important, it should not come at the expense of accuracy.

Another challenge is ensuring consistency with other biblical passages. Translators must consider how their rendering of a specific passage aligns with the broader biblical narrative and theological framework. Consistency reinforces the coherence and unity of the Scriptures.

Case Study: The UASV and Acts 20:28

The Updated American Standard Version (UASV), completed in 2022, provides an exemplary model of faithful translation in its rendering of Acts 20:28. By translating "διὰ τοῦ ἰδίου αἵματος" as "with the blood of his own Son,"[4] the UASV maintains the exact wording and theological implications of the original Greek text.

This translation aligns with other New Testament references to the atonement, preserving the connection between Jesus' sacrificial death and the salvation of believers. The UASV's commitment to accuracy and faithfulness ensures that readers can engage directly with the text and its profound theological implications.

Conclusion

The translation of Acts 20:28 exemplifies the critical importance of faithful translation. This passage's profound theological implications require a meticulous and accurate rendering that preserves the original meaning and significance. Translators must adhere to principles of literalness, contextual understanding, and theological integrity to ensure that the text remains faithful to the original.

The Updated American Standard Version (UASV) serves as a model for faithful translation, demonstrating how a commitment to accuracy and faithfulness can produce a reliable and accessible text. As we reflect on the challenges and principles of translating Acts 20:28, we are reminded of the sacred duty of translators to convey God's Word faithfully, allowing readers to engage directly with the Scriptures and their transformative power.

---

[4] Lit *with the blood of his Own*. Or, *with his own blood*.

Edward D. Andrews

CHAPTER 16 Romans 9:5 Why Are Translation Choices No Easy Matter?

Romans 9:5 presents one of the most theologically dense and textually challenging verses in the New Testament. It reads: "to whom belong the patriarchs, and from whom is the Christ according to the flesh. God, who is over all, be praised forever. Amen." (UASV). This verse addresses the identity of Christ and His relationship to God, making translation choices here particularly consequential. Translating this verse accurately requires a deep understanding of its theological implications, grammatical structure, and contextual meaning.

The Context and Importance of Romans 9:5

Romans 9 is part of Paul's letter to the Romans, where he expresses his sorrow and concern for the Israelites, his kinsmen according to the flesh. In verse 5, Paul acknowledges the privileges and heritage of the Israelites, culminating in the most significant privilege: the coming of the Messiah, Jesus Christ. This verse affirms Jesus' divine nature and His supreme position as God over all.

The Greek phrase in question, "ὁ ὢν ἐπὶ πάντων θεὸς εὐλογητὸς εἰς τοὺς αἰῶνας" (*ho ōn epi pantōn theos eulogētos eis tous aiōnas*), can be rendered in various ways, each with significant theological implications. The translation must be handled with precision to ensure that the intended meaning is faithfully conveyed.

Challenges in Translating Romans 9:5

Translating Romans 9:5 involves several challenges:

Theological Precision: The phrase "who is God over all" is a direct assertion of Christ's divinity. Translators must ensure that this declaration is clear and unambiguous.

Grammatical Structure: The Greek syntax can be complex, and choices in punctuation and word order can affect the meaning. For instance, whether the phrase "who is God over all" is taken as a doxology or a statement about Christ is critical.

Consistency with Scripture: The translation should align with other biblical references to Christ's divinity and the overall theological framework of the New Testament.

Principles for Faithful Translation

To address these challenges, translators should adhere to the following principles:

Literalness: A literal translation of key phrases such as "who is God over all" is essential to preserve the theological significance and clarity of the text.

Contextual Understanding: Translators must consider the broader context of Romans 9, understanding how verse 5 fits within Paul's argument about the privileges of Israel and the identity of the Messiah.

Theological Integrity: Maintaining the theological implications of Paul's statement is paramount. This includes the affirmation of Christ's divinity and His supreme position.

Examples of Faithful Translation

The Updated American Standard Version (UASV) renders Romans 9:5 as: "to whom belong the patriarchs, and from whom is the Christ according to the flesh. God, who is over all, be praised forever. Amen." This rendering preserves the theological depth and ambiguity inherent in the Greek text while providing a footnote: "Or, an alternative reading, Christ, who is God over all, blessed forever." This approach respects the textual variants and allows for theological reflection without imposing a definitive interpretation.

Other translations like the New American Standard Bible (NASB) and the English Standard Version (ESV) also provide literal renderings, maintaining the theological nuances and complexity of the original Greek.

The Translator's Role

The role of the translator is to convey the original text's meaning accurately, without imposing personal interpretations or biases. This responsibility is especially critical in passages like Romans 9:5, where the theological implications are profound. Translators must approach their work with a deep sense of reverence and diligence, recognizing the sacred duty of faithfully transmitting God's Word.

The Importance of Faithful Translation

Faithful translation is vital for several reasons:

Preserving Theological Truth: Accurate translation ensures that the theological truths of the Bible are maintained. In the case of Romans 9:5, this means clearly conveying Christ's divinity and supreme position.

Maintaining Scriptural Integrity: Faithful translation maintains the integrity of the Scriptures, allowing readers to engage with the text as it was originally written. This is essential for proper exegesis and theological study.

Facilitating Understanding: While accuracy is paramount, faithful translation also considers readability and clarity. A well-translated text allows readers to understand and apply its teachings more effectively.

To What Should a Good Bible Translation Be Faithful?

A good Bible translation should be faithful to several key elements:

The Original Manuscripts: The primary objective of a good translation is to accurately reflect the original Hebrew, Aramaic, and

Greek manuscripts. This involves a meticulous examination of the textual variants and the selection of the most reliable readings.

Literal Translation Philosophy: A commitment to a literal translation philosophy ensures that the words and phrases of the original text are preserved as closely as possible. This allows readers to engage directly with the inspired Scriptures.

Theological Coherence: A good translation maintains the theological coherence of the Bible. This involves ensuring that key doctrines are accurately conveyed and that the translation aligns with the overall message of Scripture.

Whom Should a Good Bible Translation Serve?

A good Bible translation should serve several key audiences:

The Faithful Reader: The primary audience for any Bible translation is the faithful reader who seeks to understand and apply God's Word. The translation should be accessible and readable while maintaining accuracy and faithfulness.

The Scholar: Scholars rely on accurate translations for exegesis, theological study, and teaching. A good translation provides the necessary tools for rigorous academic study without interpretive biases.

The Church: The church as a whole benefits from a faithful translation that preserves the integrity of the Scriptures. This allows for sound teaching, preaching, and discipleship based on the accurate transmission of God's Word.

Challenges and Solutions in Faithful Translation

Translating passages like Romans 9:5 requires navigating several challenges. One common challenge is the temptation to paraphrase or interpret the text to make it more accessible to modern readers. While readability is important, it should not come at the expense of accuracy.

Another challenge is ensuring consistency with other biblical passages. Translators must consider how their rendering of a specific passage aligns with the broader biblical narrative and theological framework. Consistency reinforces the coherence and unity of the Scriptures.

Case Study: The UASV and Romans 9:5

The Updated American Standard Version (UASV), completed in 2022, provides an exemplary model of faithful translation in its rendering of Romans 9:5. The UASV translates this verse as: "to whom belong the patriarchs, and from whom is the Christ according to the flesh. God, who is over all, be praised forever. Amen." However, it also provides a footnote that offers an alternative reading: "Or, an alternative reading, Christ, who is God over all, blessed forever." This approach respects the translation differences and allows for theological reflection to be with the reader without imposing a definitive interpretation.

This translation aligns with other New Testament references to Christ's divinity, preserving the connection between Jesus' divine nature and His supreme position. The UASV's commitment to accuracy and faithfulness ensures that readers can engage directly with the text and its profound theological implications.

CHAPTER 17 Titus 2:13 and 2 Peter 1:1 What is the Long-Debated Controversial Granville Sharp Rule?

Titus 2:13 (UASV): *"Looking for the blessed hope and the appearing of the glory of our great God and Savior Jesus Christ."*

FOOTNOTE: Or, based on grammar and context, an alternative reading could be, *"of the great God and our Savior."*

2 Peter 1:1 (UASV): *"Simon Peter, a slave and an apostle of Jesus Christ, to those who have acquired a faith as precious as ours through the righteousness of our God and Savior Jesus Christ."*

FOOTNOTE: Or, based on grammar and context, an alternative reading could be, *"of our God and the Savior Jesus Christ."*

Introduction to the Granville Sharp Rule

The Granville Sharp Rule is a grammatical principle that has sparked considerable debate among theologians and translators. Named after Granville Sharp, an 18th-century scholar, the rule addresses the use of the Greek definite article in conjunction with multiple nouns connected by the conjunction "and" (*καί, kai*). According to Sharp, when two singular personal nouns of the same case are connected by "and," and the first noun has the article while the second does not, both nouns refer to the same person.

Granville Sharp's Impact on Translation

The application of Sharp's rule has significant implications for certain New Testament passages, particularly those that pertain to the deity of Christ. Titus 2:13 and 2 Peter 1:1 are prime examples where this rule comes into play. In these verses, the identification of Jesus Christ as both God and Savior is pivotal for Christological doctrine.

Titus 2:13: Analyzing the Text

In Titus 2:13, the phrase *"the glory of our great God and Savior Jesus Christ"* is structured in a way that, according to the Granville Sharp Rule, should be understood as referring to a single person—Jesus Christ. The Greek reads: *"τῆς δόξης τοῦ μεγάλου θεοῦ καὶ σωτῆρος ἡμῶν Ἰησοῦ Χριστοῦ"* (*tēs doxēs tou megalou theou kai sōtēros hēmōn Iēsou Christou*).

Grammatical Considerations

The article *"τοῦ"* (*tou*) before *"μεγάλου θεοῦ"* (*megalou theou*, "great God") and the absence of an article before *"σωτῆρος"* (*sōtēros*, "Savior") supports the application of Sharp's rule, indicating that "God" and "Savior" refer to the same person. This construction implies that Jesus Christ is explicitly identified as both God and Savior, a crucial affirmation of His divinity.

The UASV's Translation Choices

The Updated American Standard Version (UASV) translates Titus 2:13 as: *"Looking for the blessed hope and the appearing of the glory of our great God and Savior Jesus Christ."* This rendering adheres to the Granville Sharp Rule, maintaining the theological integrity of the text. The footnote provides an alternative reading: *"of the great God and our Savior,"* acknowledging the grammatical and contextual nuances without diminishing the primary interpretation.

2 Peter 1:1: Examining the Text

In 2 Peter 1:1, the phrase *"our God and Savior Jesus Christ"* is similarly constructed to convey a unified reference to Jesus. The Greek text reads: *"τοῦ θεοῦ ἡμῶν καὶ σωτῆρος Ἰησοῦ Χριστοῦ"* (*tou theou hēmōn kai sōtēros Iēsou Christou*).

Grammatical Considerations

As with Titus 2:13, the article *"τοῦ" (tou)* appears before *"θεοῦ" (theou,* "God") but not before *"σωτῆρος" (sōtēros,* "Savior"), supporting Sharp's rule. This grammatical structure indicates that "God" and "Savior" both refer to Jesus Christ, reinforcing His divine nature.

The UASV's Translation Choices

The UASV renders 2 Peter 1:1 as: *"Simon Peter, a slave and an apostle of Jesus Christ, to those who have acquired a faith as precious as ours through the righteousness of our God and Savior Jesus Christ."* This translation adheres to Sharp's rule, emphasizing the unity of the terms "God" and "Savior" as descriptors of Jesus. The footnote provides an alternative reading: *"of our God and the Savior Jesus Christ,"* offering a nuanced understanding without compromising the primary interpretation.

Implications of the Granville Sharp Rule

The application of the Granville Sharp Rule in these passages has profound theological implications. By affirming that Jesus is referred to as both God and Savior, the rule supports key Christological doctrines, such as the deity of Christ and the Trinity. This grammatical principle helps to clarify the New Testament's teaching on the nature of Christ and His divine identity.

The Translator's Responsibility

The role of the translator is to convey the original text's meaning accurately, without imposing personal interpretations or biases. In the case of passages like Titus 2:13 and 2 Peter 1:1, the translator must carefully consider the grammatical structure and theological implications. Adherence to the Granville Sharp Rule, where applicable, ensures that the translation faithfully represents the original intent and theological depth of the text.

Challenges and Solutions in Faithful Translation

Translating complex passages like Titus 2:13 and 2 Peter 1:1 involves navigating several challenges. One common challenge is the temptation to paraphrase or interpret the text to make it more accessible to modern readers. While readability is important, it should not come at the expense of accuracy.

Another challenge is ensuring consistency with other biblical passages. Translators must consider how their rendering of a specific passage aligns with the broader biblical narrative and theological framework. Consistency reinforces the coherence and unity of the Scriptures.

The UASV's Approach

The Updated American Standard Version (UASV), completed in 2022, provides an exemplary model of faithful translation in its handling of Titus 2:13 and 2 Peter 1:1. By adhering to the Granville Sharp Rule and offering alternative readings in footnotes, the UASV maintains both the theological integrity and the grammatical accuracy of these passages. This approach allows readers to engage directly with the text while considering the broader context and interpretive nuances.

Conclusion

The translation of Titus 2:13 and 2 Peter 1:1 exemplifies the critical importance of faithful translation. These passages' profound theological implications require meticulous and accurate rendering that preserves the original meaning and significance. Translators must adhere to principles of literalness, contextual understanding, and theological integrity to ensure that the text remains faithful to the original.

The Updated American Standard Version (UASV) serves as a model for faithful translation, demonstrating how a commitment to accuracy and faithfulness can produce a reliable and accessible text. As we reflect on the challenges and principles of translating Titus 2:13 and 2 Peter 1:1, we are reminded of the sacred duty of translators to convey God's Word faithfully, allowing readers to engage directly with the Scriptures and their transformative power.

CHAPTER 18 John 2:4 Was Jesus Disrespectful to His Mother?

John 2:4 (UASV): *"And Jesus said to her, 'What have I to do with you, woman? My hour has not yet come.'"*

FOOTNOTE: The Greek does not denote any disrespect.

Introduction to the Passage

The account in John 2:1–11, where Jesus performs His first miracle at the wedding in Cana, raises questions about Jesus' interaction with His mother, Mary. In John 2:4, Jesus responds to Mary's indirect request for help with the wine shortage by saying, *"What have I to do with you, woman? My hour has not yet come."* Some readers might interpret this as a harsh or disrespectful response. However, a closer examination of the original Greek text and the cultural context reveals a different understanding.

Understanding the Greek Text

The phrase *"Τί ἐμοὶ καὶ σοί, γύναι;"* (*Ti emoi kai soi, gynai?*) is an idiomatic expression in Greek. Literally translated, it means *"What to me and to you, woman?"* This idiom was commonly used in various contexts in ancient Greek, and its tone and meaning depended heavily on the situation and relationship between the speakers.

In this context, *"woman"* (*γύναι, gynai*) was a term of respect and endearment, not one of disrespect. Jesus uses the same term when addressing Mary from the cross in John 19:26: *"Woman, behold, your son!"* Clearly, this is not a term of reproach but one of honor.

The Cultural Context

In first-century Judea, the way Jesus addressed Mary would not have been considered disrespectful. The cultural norms of the time were different from contemporary Western standards. Jesus' response to Mary reflects His awareness of His divine mission and the timing of His public ministry. By saying, *"My hour has not yet come,"* Jesus indicates that His actions are governed by divine timing rather than human intervention.

Theological Implications

Jesus' statement, *"My hour has not yet come,"* is significant in the Gospel of John. The *"hour"* refers to the appointed time of Jesus' suffering, death, and glorification. This concept is a recurring theme in John's Gospel (see John 7:30; 8:20; 12:23; 13:1; 17:1). By asserting that His hour has not yet come, Jesus is highlighting the divine schedule and purpose that govern His actions.

Translation Considerations

The UASV translates John 2:4 as: *"And Jesus said to her, 'What have I to do with you, woman? My hour has not yet come.'"* This translation preserves the literal meaning of the Greek text while also providing a footnote that clarifies the lack of disrespect inherent in the original language. The footnote serves to guide readers who might misunderstand the cultural and linguistic nuances of the passage.

Faithfulness to the Text

A faithful translation of this passage must maintain the idiomatic expression and cultural context without imposing modern sensibilities that could distort the original meaning. The goal is to convey accurately what Jesus said and how it would have been understood by His contemporaries.

Addressing Common Misunderstandings

Perceived Disrespect: Modern readers might perceive Jesus' use of *"woman"* as disrespectful. However, as noted earlier, the term was respectful and affectionate in first-century Judea.

Jesus' Relationship with Mary: Jesus' response underscores His dual role as both the obedient son and the divine Messiah. His acknowledgment of Mary's request and His subsequent miracle demonstrate His compassion and willingness to help, even as He prioritizes His divine mission.

Divine Timing: The reference to His *"hour"* emphasizes the preordained plan of salvation. Jesus' miracles and public ministry were aligned with God's timing, not human expectations.

Implications for Bible Translation

Translators must balance literal accuracy with cultural and contextual understanding. In John 2:4, preserving the original idiom is crucial, but so is providing explanatory notes that help modern readers grasp the meaning and tone of Jesus' words. The UASV's approach exemplifies this balance, offering both a literal translation and a clarifying footnote.

Conclusion

In John 2:4, Jesus' response to His mother, Mary, is not one of disrespect but one that reflects His divine mission and the timing of His ministry. The Greek idiom used by Jesus and the cultural context of the time reveal a tone of respect and honor. The UASV's translation and accompanying footnote help modern readers understand the true nature of this interaction, preserving the integrity and depth of the original text.

A faithful translation of this passage, like that provided by the UASV, ensures that readers receive an accurate and respectful rendering of Jesus' words. By maintaining the literal meaning and offering contextual explanations, translators can convey the richness of the biblical narrative and its theological significance.

Edward D. Andrews

CHAPTER 19 Mark 10:15 Over and Under Translation of the Bible

Mark 10:15 (UASV): *"Truly I say to you, whoever does not receive the kingdom of God like a child will never enter into it."*

FOOTNOTE: The Greek construction of *(οὐ μὴ εἰσέλθῃ)* is literally "not not should enter." This is forever true: as long as the person does not receive the kingdom of God like a child, he or she will never by no means, in any way, enter the kingdom of God.

Introduction

Translating the Bible involves more than simply converting words from one language to another. It requires a careful balancing act to ensure that the translation is both faithful to the original text and comprehensible to contemporary readers. This balance is crucial in avoiding the extremes of over-translation and under-translation, which can distort the intended meaning of the Scriptures. Mark 10:15 serves as an excellent case study for exploring these concepts.

Understanding Over-Translation and Under-Translation

Over-Translation: This occurs when translators add explanatory words or phrases to the text, aiming to clarify the meaning but potentially imposing their interpretations. Over-translation can lead to a loss of the original text's ambiguity or nuance, which is essential for allowing readers to engage with the text directly.

Under-Translation: Conversely, under-translation happens when translators omit necessary context or fail to capture the full meaning of the original text. This can result in a translation that is too literal or simplistic, leaving readers without sufficient understanding of the text's deeper implications.

Mark 10:15: Analyzing the Text

In Mark 10:15, Jesus makes a profound statement about the nature of receiving the kingdom of God. The verse reads: *"Truly I say to you, whoever does not receive the kingdom of God like a child will never enter into it."* The Greek phrase *"οὐ μὴ εἰσέλθῃ"* (*ou mē eiselthē*) is an emphatic negation, conveying the absolute impossibility of entering the kingdom without the requisite childlike reception.

The Greek Construction

The Greek construction *"οὐ μὴ"* is a strong double negative, emphasizing that the action will never occur under any circumstances. The literal rendering *"not not should enter"* highlights the impossibility, which the UASV footnote clarifies: *"This is forever true: as long as the person does not receive the kingdom of God like a child, he or she will never by no means, in any way, enter the kingdom of God."*

Avoiding Over-Translation

In translating Mark 10:15, it is essential to avoid over-translation that might obscure the text's simplicity and forcefulness. For example, adding explanatory phrases about what it means to *"receive the kingdom of God like a child"* could impose an interpretive layer that the original text does not specify. The UASV's straightforward translation preserves the verse's directness and impact, allowing readers to ponder the meaning of childlike reception themselves.

Avoiding Under-Translation

At the same time, under-translation can leave the verse's emphatic negation unclear. A too-literal rendering like *"not not should enter"* might confuse readers unfamiliar with Greek syntax. By providing a footnote that explains the strong negation, the UASV ensures that the verse's forcefulness is communicated without compromising its literal fidelity.

The Role of Footnotes

Footnotes play a crucial role in balancing the need for literal translation and the necessity of clarity. In Mark 10:15, the UASV footnote explains the Greek construction, helping readers understand the verse's full implications without altering the text itself. This approach maintains the translation's accuracy while providing necessary context.

Theological Implications

The statement in Mark 10:15 has significant theological implications. Jesus emphasizes the importance of humility and receptiveness in entering the kingdom of God. By preserving the text's literal meaning and providing explanatory footnotes, translators help readers grasp these profound truths.

The Translator's Responsibility

Translators bear a significant responsibility in rendering the Bible accurately and faithfully. They must navigate the challenges of over-translation and under-translation, ensuring that the text remains true to the original while being accessible to modern readers. This balance requires a deep understanding of the original languages, the cultural and historical context, and the theological significance of the text.

Examples of Faithful Translation

The UASV Approach: The Updated American Standard Version (UASV), completed in 2022, exemplifies a commitment to literal translation philosophy. In Mark 10:15, the UASV translates the verse as: *"Truly I say to you, whoever does not receive the kingdom of God like a child will never enter into it."* The accompanying footnote provides clarity on the Greek construction, ensuring that readers understand the emphatic nature of Jesus' statement without altering the text.

The Importance of Literal Translation Philosophy

Adhering to a literal translation philosophy is crucial for maintaining the integrity of the Scriptures. This approach ensures that translators do not impose their interpretations on the text but rather convey what the original authors intended. By doing so, they allow readers to engage directly with the Word of God, discerning its meaning and applying it to their lives.

Conclusion

The translation of Mark 10:15 highlights the critical balance between over-translation and under-translation. Faithful translators must strive to maintain the text's literal meaning while providing necessary context and clarity. The UASV's approach to Mark 10:15 exemplifies this balance, offering a literal translation with explanatory footnotes that help readers grasp the full implications of Jesus' statement.

By adhering to a literal translation philosophy, translators fulfill their sacred duty to convey God's Word faithfully. This commitment ensures that readers receive the Scriptures as they were originally given, allowing them to engage directly with the divine message and its transformative power.

SECTION FIVE: The Reliability of Our Bibles

The reliability of our Bibles is a topic that has been scrutinized and debated for centuries. While this section cannot cover every aspect of this extensive subject, it aims to provide a thorough understanding of why we can trust the Bible we have today. Our focus will be on the integrity of the original manuscripts, the meticulous process of textual transmission, and the accuracy of literal translations that serve as mirror-like reflections of the original texts in English.

The Integrity of the Original Manuscripts

The Bible's original manuscripts, written by inspired human authors under the guidance of the Holy Spirit, have long been regarded as the infallible Word of God. Despite the absence of the autographs (the original documents), the numerous copies made by scribes over the centuries have provided a robust textual foundation. The sheer volume of available manuscripts—particularly for the New Testament—is unparalleled in ancient literature, giving scholars a vast reservoir of data to compare and analyze.

The Process of Textual Transmission

Textual transmission refers to the process of copying and disseminating the biblical texts throughout history. This process was not without its challenges, including human error and occasional intentional alterations. However, the vast number of manuscripts available allows for a comprehensive comparison, enabling scholars to identify and correct these discrepancies. The science of textual criticism has made significant strides in reconstructing the most accurate text possible.

The Old Testament

The transmission of the Old Testament text was meticulously overseen by Jewish scribes. The Masoretes, in particular, played a crucial role in preserving the text through their detailed system of checks and balances, which included counting the number of letters and words in each book. The discovery of the Dead Sea Scrolls—dating from the third century B.C.E. to the first century C.E.—has confirmed the reliability of the Masoretic Text, showing remarkable consistency over a millennium of transmission.

The New Testament

The New Testament boasts an unprecedented number of manuscripts, with over 5,800 Greek manuscripts, 10,000 Latin manuscripts, and thousands more in other languages. This abundance of material allows for rigorous cross-checking. Early church fathers' quotations and lectionaries further supplement this body of evidence, ensuring that the text we have today closely aligns with the original writings.

The Role of Literal Translations

Literal translations aim to preserve the exact words and phrasing of the original texts, striving for word-for-word accuracy. These translations provide a direct and faithful representation of the original languages, allowing readers to engage with the Bible in its most authentic form. The *Updated American Standard Version* (UASV), completed in 2022, exemplifies this commitment to literal translation, offering a precise reflection of the original Hebrew, Aramaic, and Greek texts.

Addressing Common Concerns

Variants and Their Impact

One of the most common concerns regarding the reliability of the Bible is the presence of textual variants. While there are numerous variants among the thousands of manuscripts, the vast majority are minor and do not affect fundamental doctrines or teachings. Variants often involve spelling differences, word order, or the inclusion or omission of articles. Through textual criticism, scholars can ascertain the most likely original readings, ensuring the text's overall integrity remains intact.

Alleged Contradictions

Another frequent issue raised by skeptics is the presence of alleged contradictions within the Bible. A careful examination of these apparent contradictions often reveals harmonizing solutions. Understanding the historical and cultural context, the intended audience, and the literary genre of each book can resolve many of these issues. Additionally, recognizing the Bible's progressive revelation helps to explain differences in emphasis and detail across the biblical narrative.

The Testimony of Archaeology

Archaeological discoveries have consistently corroborated the historical and cultural contexts described in the Bible. From the ruins of ancient cities mentioned in the Old Testament to inscriptions bearing the names of New Testament figures, archaeology has provided tangible evidence supporting the Bible's reliability. These findings affirm the historical accuracy of the biblical record, reinforcing our confidence in the Scriptures.

The Enduring Impact of the Bible

The Bible's influence on individuals and societies throughout history is a testament to its enduring reliability. Its teachings have shaped laws, ethics, and cultural norms, demonstrating its transformative power. The Bible's ability to withstand scrutiny, inspire faith, and guide moral behavior speaks to its divine origin and trustworthy nature.

While this section cannot address every aspect of the Bible's reliability, it provides a comprehensive overview of why we can trust

THE CHALLENGE OF TRANSLATING TRUTH

the Scriptures we have today. The meticulous process of textual transmission, the abundance of manuscript evidence, the precision of literal translations, and the corroborative testimony of archaeology all affirm the Bible's trustworthiness. As believers, we can have confidence that the Word of God we hold in our hands is a faithful and accurate reflection of the original inspired texts, allowing us to engage with the divine message with assurance and reverence.

CHAPTER 20 The Author's Intended Meaning Should Not Always Be Immediately Clear

In the journey of Bible translation, one of the critical issues that arise is whether the author's intended meaning should always be immediately clear to the reader. This question strikes at the heart of translation philosophy and challenges the translator's approach to rendering the sacred texts.

The Nature of Biblical Texts

Biblical texts, originating from ancient Hebrew, Aramaic, and Greek, often contain layers of meaning, cultural nuances, and idiomatic expressions that are foreign to modern readers. These elements pose significant challenges for translators who strive to be faithful to the original text while making it comprehensible to contemporary audiences.

For instance, the use of parables by Jesus was a deliberate choice to convey deeper truths in a manner that required contemplation and spiritual insight. In Matthew 13:13–15 (UASV), Jesus explains the purpose of parables: *"Therefore I speak to them in parables, because while seeing they do not see, and while hearing they do not hear, nor do they understand. In their case the prophecy of Isaiah is being fulfilled, which says, 'You will keep on hearing, but will not understand; you will keep on seeing, but will not perceive.'"*

The Role of the Translator

A translator's primary duty is to render the text accurately and faithfully, preserving the original meaning intended by the authors under divine inspiration. This involves a delicate balance between literal translation and dynamic equivalence, where the latter aims to convey thought-for-thought rather than word-for-word.

The Updated American Standard Version (UASV), completed in 2022, exemplifies this commitment to accuracy. By maintaining a literal translation philosophy, it ensures that readers are provided with a text as close to the original as possible, allowing them to engage deeply with the Scriptures and uncover the intended meanings through study and reflection.

Clarity and Interpretation

While clarity is an essential goal in translation, it should not come at the expense of fidelity to the original text. Some passages are inherently complex and ambiguous, reflecting the depth and richness of the biblical message. Simplifying these passages can result in a loss of meaning and nuance.

For example, in 2 Peter 3:16 (UASV), Peter acknowledges the complexity of Paul's writings: *"as also in all his letters, speaking in them of these things, in which are some things hard to understand, which the untaught and unstable distort, as they do also the rest of the Scriptures, to their own destruction."* This acknowledgment underscores the need for careful study and interpretation rather than oversimplification.

The Responsibility of the Reader

The responsibility of understanding the text ultimately lies with the reader, guided by the Holy Spirit and proper hermeneutical methods. Translators should not assume the role of interpreters by inserting their own understanding into the translation. Instead, they should provide a faithful rendering that allows readers to engage with the text and discover its meanings.

The Historical-Grammatical Method of interpretation, which emphasizes understanding the original context, grammar, and syntax, is crucial in this process. This method respects the text's integrity and encourages readers to delve deeper into the historical and cultural backgrounds of the passages.

Examples of Translation Challenges

Consider the Greek phrase *"τὰ βάθη τοῦ θεοῦ"* in 1 Corinthians 2:10 (UASV), translated as *"the depths of God."* This phrase conveys profound theological concepts that require careful contemplation and study. A dynamic equivalent might simplify it to *"God's deep truths,"* but this loses the evocative imagery of the original.

Another example is found in Romans 3:25 (UASV), which speaks of Jesus as *"a propitiation in His blood."* The term *"propitiation"* is a technical theological term that encapsulates the idea of atonement and satisfaction of divine justice. Replacing it with a more generic term like *"sacrifice"* would dilute its specific theological implications.

Conclusion

In conclusion, the author's intended meaning should not always be immediately clear, as the depth and richness of the biblical texts require contemplation and study. Translators must balance clarity with fidelity, ensuring that the original meaning is preserved while allowing readers to engage deeply with the Scriptures. The responsibility of understanding the text ultimately lies with the reader, guided by proper hermeneutical methods and the Holy Spirit.

The UASV, with its commitment to literal translation, provides an exemplary model of how this balance can be achieved, ensuring that readers are given the authentic Word of God, unfiltered by interpretive biases. This approach respects the sacred duty of translation and upholds the integrity of the biblical message, allowing it to speak with its full depth and power to all who seek its truths.

THE CHALLENGE OF TRANSLATING TRUTH

CHAPTER 21 Why Have Modern Bible Translation Removed Words, Phrases, Sentences, Even Whole Verses?

As some Christians have been studying their King James Version and comparing it to other modern translations, they have discovered that in the King James Version there are verses that these other translators removed. Examples include Luke 17:36, Matthew 18:11, and Matthew 23:14. Many uninformed or willfully blind King James Onlyists have used these verses to misinform readers of the King James Version. Below will be a detailed reason why they are missing from the modern Bible translations, except the Holman Christian Standard Bible and the New American Standard Bible. Thereafter, we will offer more technical internal and external evidence as to why.

The Warning

Deuteronomy 4:2; 12:32, Updated American Standard Version (UASV), states:

2 *"You shall not add to the word which I am commanding you, nor take away from it, that you may keep the commandments of Jehovah your God which I command you."*
32 *"Everything that I command you, you shall be careful to do; you shall not add to nor take away from it."*

Revelation 22:18–19, UASV, also cautions:

18 *"I testify to everyone who hears the words of the prophecy of this book: if anyone adds to them, God will add to him the plagues which are written in this book;*

19 *and if anyone takes away from the words of the book of this prophecy, God will take away his part from the tree of life and out of the holy city, which are written in this book."*

These are the verses that the King James Version Onlyists use to misinform the King James Version reader. First, it is true that if one removes a part of the Bible that was in the originals, it would be a catastrophic matter for that person or persons. Second, I would argue, as would the modern-day translators, that Luke 17:36, Matthew 18:11, and Matthew 23:14 were not in the originals; they were added by later copyists who are actually the ones who added to God's Word and so, they face the above judgment. Third, I would further point out that you cannot add what was never there in the first place. Let us see why the modern-day Bibles are not lacking these verses.

Because this may be the first time some are hearing that there are certain words, phrases, sentences, even whole verses that are found in the King James Version and other older translations that are not authentic, i.e., they were not in the original.

Copying Manuscripts

Some are still not aware that no Bible translator has had access to the originals of the New Testament when making their translations because they have not been in existence for almost 2,000 years. Even if they were discovered, we could never ascertain that they were the originals unless they were autographed by Matthew, Mark, Luke, John, James, Peter, or Jude.

Over time, the process of copying manuscripts by hand led to the introduction of variations. These variations can be categorized into accidental errors and intentional alterations. Accidental errors include misspellings, word omissions, or duplications due to the scribe's fatigue or distraction. Intentional alterations might involve harmonizing gospel accounts, clarifying ambiguous passages, or making doctrinal corrections. This is a natural outcome of the human involvement in the transmission process, not a reflection of God's Word being flawed.

THE CHALLENGE OF TRANSLATING TRUTH

The Case of Luke 17:36 and Other Verses

Luke 17:36 in the King James Version reads: *"Two men shall be in the field; the one shall be taken, and the other left."* However, this verse is absent from many modern translations. The primary reason for its exclusion is the lack of manuscript evidence. Early and reliable Greek manuscripts do not include this verse, indicating it was likely a later addition.

Similarly, Matthew 18:11, which says, *"For the Son of man is come to save that which was lost,"* is missing from many modern versions. The earliest and most reliable manuscripts do not contain this verse, suggesting it was added by later scribes to harmonize with Luke 19:10.

Matthew 23:14, which reads, *"Woe unto you, scribes and Pharisees, hypocrites! for ye devour widows' houses, and for a pretense make long prayer: therefore ye shall receive the greater damnation,"* is another verse absent in many modern translations. The verse is absent in the earliest and most reliable Greek manuscripts, which points to its addition in later texts.

Reconstructing the Original Text

New Testament textual scholars have over 5,836 Greek manuscripts, not to mention ancient versions such as Latin, Coptic, Syriac, Armenian, Georgian, and Gothic, which number into the tens of thousands. We have many early and reliable manuscripts in Greek and the versions, a good number that cover almost the entire New Testament dating within 100 years of the originals. Therefore, reconstructing the original Greek New Testament is not only realistic but is now a reality.

The science of textual criticism aims to reconstruct the original text of the New Testament as accurately as possible. Textual critics examine the manuscript evidence, considering factors such as the age, geographical distribution, and textual family of the manuscripts. They also evaluate internal evidence, such as the context and style of the author, to determine the most likely original reading.

The Role of Early Church Fathers

The writings of early Church Fathers provide valuable insight into the text of the New Testament. These Church Fathers, such as Justin Martyr, Irenaeus, Clement of Alexandria, and Origen, quoted extensively from the New Testament in their writings. By examining their quotations, textual critics can cross-reference these with existing manuscripts to verify the authenticity of certain readings.

For instance, when a passage quoted by an early Church Father is absent in the earliest Greek manuscripts but present in later ones, it suggests that the passage might have been a later addition. Conversely, if a passage is consistently quoted by early Church Fathers and present in early manuscripts, it supports the passage's authenticity.

Addressing Misconceptions

One common misconception is that modern translators are removing verses to undermine the integrity of the Bible. However, the goal of modern translations is to faithfully represent the original text. When verses are removed, it is because evidence suggests they were not part of the original manuscripts. This process is not about taking away from God's Word but about preserving its authenticity.

Some King James Onlyists argue that modern translations are corrupt because they omit these verses. However, these omissions are based on careful scholarly work and manuscript evidence. The aim is to present the text as it was originally written, without the later additions that crept into the transmission process.

The Trustworthiness of Modern Translations

The entire Bible that we have today—the critical translation of the Hebrew Old Testament and the Greek New Testament—are mirror-like reflections of the originals. All translations that remain faithful to the original are reliable. New Testament textual scholars have over 5,836 Greek manuscripts, and many early and reliable manuscripts in Greek and the versions, a good number that cover almost the entire New Testament dating within 100 years of the originals. Therefore, reconstructing the original Greek New Testament is realistic and a reality.

We should note that 90% of the Hebrew Old Testament text is without significant variation and 93% of the Greek New Testament text is without significant variation. The work of hundreds of textual scholars from the days of Desiderius Erasmus have given their entire lives to the restoration of the Greek New Testament. Therefore, textual scholars only need to focus their attention on this very small 7% of significant textual variants. These variants that have been corrected have not undermined the Word of God; rather, they highlight and stress the fact that God has preserved His Word through restoration.

Conclusion

In conclusion, the removal of certain words, phrases, sentences, and even whole verses in modern Bible translations is not an act of diminishing God's Word but an effort to restore it to its original form. The goal is to give the Bible readers what God said by way of His human authors, not what a translator thinks God meant in its place. The meaning of a word is the responsibility of the interpreter, not the translator. Thus, modern translations strive to be accurate and faithful to the original text, ensuring that readers can engage directly with the Scriptures and their transformative power.

Edward D. Andrews

CHAPTER 22 Mistakes Were Made in Copying God's Word, But Was the Purity of the Bible Text Threatened? Were These Serious Enough to Ruin the Message of the Bible?

Throughout history, the transmission of the Bible has been a meticulous yet human endeavor. The reality that mistakes were made in copying God's Word is undeniable. However, the critical question remains: Were these errors serious enough to threaten the purity of the Bible's text and ruin its message?

Historical Context of Textual Transmission

The history of biblical transmission reveals a profound dedication among scribes to preserve the integrity of the text. Dionysius of Corinth, a second-century Christian overseer, lamented the alterations made to his own writings, which he attributed to the "apostles of the devil." He noted, *"For I wrote letters when the brethren requested me to write. And these letters the apostles of the devil have filled with tares, taking away some things and adding others."* This acknowledgment underscores the reality that tampering with sacred texts was recognized and lamented even in ancient times.

Tertullian, another early Christian writer, documented similar practices by Marcion, who *"expressly and openly used the knife, not the pen,"* to excise portions of the Scriptures that did not conform to his doctrinal views. Despite these attempts, the overall preservation of the biblical message was remarkably successful.

The Extent of Variants

Modern textual criticism has identified over 400,000 variants in the New Testament manuscripts alone. This number can be alarming at first glance, but it requires careful contextualization. These variants are spread across approximately 5,800 Greek manuscripts, and the vast majority are minor, such as spelling errors, word order changes, or other inconsequential differences.

Bart D. Ehrman, a prominent textual critic, often highlights the large number of variants to question the reliability of the New Testament. However, it's essential to understand that the vast majority of these variants do not affect the meaning or theology of the text. Instead, they reflect the scribes' meticulous efforts to copy texts accurately, albeit with human errors.

Preservation Through Restoration

The preservation of the biblical text has been a process of restoration rather than miraculous preservation. God did not supernaturally prevent scribes from making errors, but He ensured that the faithful transmission of His Word would be possible through diligent scholarship. Over centuries, textual critics have compared thousands of manuscripts to restore the original text as closely as possible.

For instance, the Hebrew Scriptures, copied meticulously by the Sopherim, contained around 815,140 Hebrew letters. The care taken by these scribes was extraordinary, yet not infallible. Variants existed, but the overall message remained intact. The discovery of the Dead Sea Scrolls, which date back to the second century B.C.E., confirmed that the text of the Hebrew Bible had remained remarkably consistent over a thousand years.

The Role of the Masoretes

The Masoretes, working between the sixth and tenth centuries C.E., played a crucial role in preserving the Hebrew text. They developed a system of vowel points and accent marks to ensure accurate pronunciation and interpretation. Despite their meticulous efforts, they did not eliminate all variants. However, their work significantly contributed to the stability and uniformity of the Hebrew Bible.

How We Got the Hebrew Old Testament:

Earliest Translated Versions:

1. **The Samaritan Pentateuch:**
    - **Origin:** Developed by the Samaritans, who mixed Israelite worship with pagan practices. This version includes only the first five books of the Hebrew Scriptures (Torah).
    - **Script:** Written in the Samaritan script, which evolved from ancient Hebrew script.
    - **Date:** Estimated creation between the 4th to 2nd centuries BCE.
    - **Content and Variations:** Contains about 6,000 variations from the standard Hebrew Masoretic text, most minor, but still valuable for textual comparison. However, existing manuscript copies date mostly from the 13th century CE or later.

2. **The Aramaic Targums:**
    - **Purpose:** As Aramaic became the vernacular among Jews in Persian territories post-Nehemiah, these were necessary to translate or paraphrase the Hebrew Scriptures during public readings.
    - **Nature:** Not direct translations but interpretations or paraphrases, providing cultural and interpretative context to the Hebrew text.
    - **Date:** Final form likely no earlier than the 5th century CE.

3. **The Greek Septuagint (LXX):**

THE CHALLENGE OF TRANSLATING TRUTH

- **Origin:** Began around 280 BCE by 72 Jewish scholars in Alexandria, Egypt, for the Greek-speaking Jewish community.
- **Significance:** It's the first major translation from Hebrew to another language. It was widely used by both Jews and early Christians.
- **Divine Name:** Originally included the Tetragrammaton (the four Hebrew letters representing God's name), which was later altered to Kyrios (Lord) or Theos (God).
- **Manuscripts:** Fragments on papyrus, like the Fouad Papyri, show the use of the divine name in Hebrew characters within the Greek text. Many manuscripts exist in both uncial (large capital letters) and minuscule (cursive) scripts.

4. **The Latin Vulgate:**
   - **Creation:** By Jerome around 390-405 CE, translating directly from Hebrew and Greek.
   - **Purpose:** To provide a common Latin version for Western Christendom, understandable to the general populace.
   - **Content:** Included apocryphal books but distinguished them from canonical texts.

The Hebrew-Language Texts:

1. **The Sopherim (Scribes):**
   - **Role:** Began copying Hebrew Scriptures from Ezra's time; they sometimes made textual alterations, which Jesus criticized.

2. **The Masora and Masoretic Text:**
   - **Masoretes:** Successors to the Sopherim who added vowel points and accents to the consonantal text for pronunciation aid, without changing the text itself.

- **Masora:** Marginal notes detailing textual alterations made by the Sopherim, including changes to divine names and other textual emendations.
- **Schools:** Babylonian, Palestinian, and Tiberian, with the Tiberian system becoming standard.

3. **The Dead Sea Scrolls:**
   - **Discovery:** Began in 1947 near the Dead Sea, providing texts dating back to the 2nd century BCE.
   - **Significance:** Show remarkable agreement with the Masoretic text in terms of content, despite minor spelling or grammatical differences.

The Refined Hebrew Text:

- **Historical Editions:**
  - **Second Rabbinic Bible:** Edited by Jacob ben Chayyim (1524-25) was a standard for centuries.
  - **Critical Study:** Pioneered by scholars like Benjamin Kennicott and J. B. de Rossi in the 18th century, leading to more refined editions.
- **Modern Editions:**
  - **Biblia Hebraica:** By Rudolf Kittel, first edition 1906, with subsequent editions improving upon the text using older, more accurate Masoretic manuscripts like those from the Ben Asher tradition.

This comprehensive approach to understanding the transmission and preservation of the Hebrew Old Testament text illustrates a meticulous process involving translation, copying, textual criticism, and scholarly refinement over centuries.

The Greek New Testament

The Greek New Testament manuscripts also exhibit a high degree of care in copying. The earliest manuscripts, such as those from the second and third centuries, show a variety of hands, from professional scribes to literate amateurs. Despite this range, the core message of the New Testament has been preserved through careful comparative analysis by textual critics.

One of the most significant projects in this regard has been the ongoing work on the Updated American Standard Version (UASV). Completed in 2022, the UASV draws on the most reliable Greek and Hebrew texts, incorporating insights from the latest textual research. The UASV aims to present a text that is as close as possible to the original autographs, reflecting the original wording and meaning intended by the biblical authors.

No Miraculous Preservation but Rather Preservation and Restoration

1 Peter 1:25 and Isaiah 40:8 are often taken by the charismatics, the King James Version Onlyists, and those in the unknowing to mean that God's Word has gone unchanged since the original were written. They believe in miraculous preservation, which is biblically untrue and not the case in reality because there are hundreds of thousands of textual variants in tens of thousands of Hebrew and Greek manuscripts. What we have is the copyists preserving the texts as best as they could.

Scribal Skills

The quality and precision of these copies often depended on the scribe's skill. Manuscripts can exhibit different handwriting styles, indicating the diversity of scribes involved in their copying:

The Common Hand: Sometimes, it can be tough to differentiate a badly made "documentary" handwriting from a regular one. However, typically, common handwriting shows the effort of someone with limited Greek-writing skills.

The Documentary Hand: These scribes were often accustomed to writing documents, such as business records or minor official documents. Their work is characterized by non-uniform lettering, with the initial letter on each line often larger than the rest. The lines of letters may not be even.

The Reformed Documentary Hand: This term refers to scribes who were aware they were copying a literary work rather than a mere document. Their work often exhibits more care and a slightly higher degree of uniformity than the basic documentary hand.

Professional Bookhand: Some manuscripts were clearly copied by professional scribes skilled in producing literary texts. An example is the Gospel codex known as P4+64+67, which showcases well-crafted calligraphy, paragraph markings, double columns, and punctuation.

How We Got the Greek Text of the New Testament:

Transmission:

1. **Inspiration and Original Writing:**
   - The New Testament writings are considered by Christians to be inspired by the Holy Spirit. This means that the original authors, like Paul, John, or Peter, were guided by divine influence in their composition. This process is described in 2 Peter 1:21 where it states that "men spoke from God as they were carried along by the Holy Spirit."

2. **Manuscript Copying:**
   - After the originals were written, they were copied by hand. This copying was not under the same divine inspiration. Therefore, while the original texts were considered inerrant by believers, the copies made by scribes could contain errors due to human limitations.

Corruption:

1. **Unintentional Errors:**
   - **Orthographic Variants:** Simple spelling mistakes or misunderstandings of the text due to similar sounding words in Greek.

- **Omissions or Additions:** Sometimes, scribes would inadvertently omit words or lines, or add them based on what they thought should be there or what they remembered from memory.
- **Transpositions:** Words or letters might be written in a different order.

2. **Intentional Changes:**
   - **Harmonizations:** Scribes might adjust texts to make them consistent with parallel accounts in other Gospels or with Old Testament passages.
   - **Theological Emendations:** Changes made to clarify or emphasize theological points, or sometimes to protect the text against heretical interpretations.

Types of Scribal Hands:

- **The Common Hand:**
  - Reflects the work of less skilled or less literate scribes. The handwriting might be sloppy, letters might be uneven, and there could be frequent mistakes due to the scribe's limited proficiency in Greek.

- **The Documentary Hand:**
  - Used by scribes familiar with writing documents like contracts or letters. The writing might not be aesthetically pleasing but functional. Letters might vary in size, especially with the first letter of a line being larger, and lines might not be straight.

- **The Reformed Documentary Hand:**
  - Indicates a scribe who recognized the text's literary value, aiming for better legibility and uniformity than a purely documentary hand but not reaching the skill level of a professional.

- **Professional Bookhand:**

- Employed by those trained in calligraphy for literary works. These manuscripts would exhibit careful lettering, use of spacing, punctuation, and other features for clarity and beauty. An example is the early codex P4+64+67, which shows advanced scribal practices.

Restoration:

- **Textual Criticism:**
    - From the 18th century onwards, scholars like Johann Jakob Griesbach, Karl Lachmann, Constantin von Tischendorf, Brooke Foss Westcott and Fenton John Anthony Hort, Eberhard Nestle, Kurt and Barbara Aland, and Bruce M. Metzger have worked on reconstructing the original text of the New Testament.
    - They compare thousands of manuscripts, versions, and quotations by early Church Fathers to discern the most likely original readings. Their work involves:
        - **Collation:** Comparing manuscripts to note variants.
        - **Textual Analysis:** Evaluating these variants based on external (manuscript age, geographical distribution) and internal (scribal habits, theological tendencies) evidence.
        - **Eclectic Editions:** Producing texts that blend readings from various manuscripts believed to best represent the original text.

This scholarly endeavor continues today with the use of digital tools and broader manuscript access, striving to get closer to the original wording of the New Testament texts while acknowledging the human elements in their transmission.

Theological Implications

The theological implications of textual variants must be carefully considered. While some variants are theologically significant, none undermine the core doctrines of the Christian faith. For example, the doctrine of the Trinity, the deity of Christ, and the resurrection are all well-supported by a multitude of texts, even when variants are taken into account.

Eminent scholars such as F. F. Bruce and Bruce Metzger have argued that the New Testament is the best-attested document from the ancient world. The wealth of manuscripts, early translations, and quotations in patristic writings provides a robust foundation for reconstructing the original text.

Conclusion

In conclusion, while mistakes were indeed made in the copying of God's Word, these errors were not serious enough to threaten the purity of the Bible's text or ruin its message. The dedicated efforts of scribes, scholars, and textual critics have ensured that we have a text that is, in essence, a mirror-like reflection of the original writings. The UASV, completed in 2022, stands as a testament to this ongoing commitment to faithful biblical translation. Through diligent scholarship and divine providence, the Bible remains a trustworthy and authoritative guide for faith and practice.

CHAPTER 23 How the Bible Survived Careless and Even Deceitful Bible Copyists?

The transmission of the Bible through centuries has been a journey marked by meticulous care as well as instances of carelessness and even deceit among copyists. Despite these challenges, the Bible has survived with its core message intact, demonstrating the remarkable resilience and divine preservation of God's Word.

Historical Context of Biblical Copying

The process of copying the Bible began with the Jewish scribes, whose reverence for the text led them to develop stringent methods to preserve its accuracy. These scribes, known as the Sopherim, meticulously counted every letter and word to ensure precise duplication. Their dedication was extraordinary, but human errors were inevitable.

With the spread of Christianity, the task of copying the New Testament manuscripts fell to a broader range of scribes, from highly trained professionals to literate but less skilled individuals. This diversity in scribal quality contributed to the variations found in the manuscripts.

Nature and Extent of Variants

Modern textual criticism has revealed that there are over 400,000 textual variants among the New Testament manuscripts. At first glance, this number may appear alarming, but it is important to understand that the majority of these variants are minor and do not affect the overall message of the Bible. They include differences in spelling, word order, and minor omissions or additions.

Bart D. Ehrman, a well-known textual critic, often emphasizes the number of variants to suggest that the New Testament text is unreliable. However, his conclusions are disputed by many scholars who point out that these variants do not undermine the essential teachings of Christianity. In fact, the vast majority of variants are inconsequential and can be easily identified and corrected through comparative analysis.

Intentional Changes by Copyists

In addition to unintentional errors, there were instances where copyists made intentional changes to the text. These changes were often motivated by doctrinal disputes or the desire to clarify the meaning of a passage. For example, some scribes altered texts to support particular theological positions or to harmonize discrepancies between parallel accounts in the Gospels.

One notable example is the Johannine Comma (1 John 5:7–8), a passage that appears in later manuscripts but is absent in the earliest Greek texts. This addition, which explicitly supports the doctrine of the Trinity, was likely inserted by a scribe who wished to strengthen the scriptural basis for this doctrine. Modern textual critics, recognizing this as a later addition, have excluded it from most contemporary translations.

The Role of the Masoretes

The Masoretes, Jewish scribes working between the sixth and tenth centuries C.E., played a crucial role in preserving the Hebrew text of the Old Testament. They developed a system of vowel points and accents to standardize pronunciation and ensure accurate transmission. Despite their meticulous efforts, variants still existed. However, the Masoretes' work significantly contributed to the stability and uniformity of the Hebrew Bible.

The Greek New Testament

The Greek New Testament manuscripts also exhibit a high degree of care in copying. The earliest manuscripts, such as those from the second and third centuries, show a variety of hands, from professional scribes to literate amateurs. Despite this range, the core message of the New Testament has been preserved through careful comparative analysis by textual critics.

One of the most significant projects in this regard has been the ongoing work on the Updated American Standard Version (UASV). Completed in 2022, the UASV draws on the most reliable Greek and Hebrew texts, incorporating insights from the latest textual research. The UASV aims to present a text that is as close as possible to the original autographs, reflecting the original wording and meaning intended by the biblical authors.

Theological Implications

Theological implications of textual variants must be carefully considered. While some variants are theologically significant, none undermine the core doctrines of the Christian faith. For example, the doctrine of the Trinity, the deity of Christ, and the resurrection are all well-supported by a multitude of texts, even when variants are taken into account.

Eminent scholars such as F. F. Bruce and Bruce Metzger have argued that the New Testament is the best-attested document from the ancient world. The wealth of manuscripts, early translations, and quotations in patristic writings provides a robust foundation for reconstructing the original text.

Conclusion

The survival of the Bible through centuries of copying, despite the presence of careless and even deceitful copyists, is a testament to the divine preservation of God's Word. While human errors and intentional changes have occurred, the core message of the Bible remains intact and reliable. The diligent work of textual critics and the

THE CHALLENGE OF TRANSLATING TRUTH

discovery of ancient manuscripts have allowed for the restoration of the original text, ensuring that the Bible we have today faithfully reflects the words of its inspired authors.

As we continue to study and translate the Bible, it is essential to remain committed to accuracy and faithfulness, recognizing the sacred responsibility of conveying God's Word to future generations. The Updated American Standard Version (UASV), completed in 2022, stands as a testament to this ongoing commitment, providing a reliable and accessible text for all who seek to understand and apply the teachings of Scripture.

Bibliography

Aland, K. a. (1987). *The Text of the New Testament.* Grand Rapids: Eerdmans.

Aland, K. a. (1987). *The Text of the New Testament.* Grand Rapids: Eerdmans.

Andrews, E. (2018). *THE EARLY CHRISTIAN COPYISTS OF THE NEW TESTAMENT: The Making and Copying of the New Testament Books.* Cambridge: Christian Publishing House.

Andrews, E. (2019). *Misrepresenting Jesus: Debunking Bart D. Ehrman's Misquoting Jesus [Fourth Edition].* Cambridge: Christian Publishing House.

Andrews, E. (2020). *FROM SPOKEN WORDS TO SACRED TEXTS: Introduction-Intermediate New Testament Textual Studies.* Cambridge: Christian Publishing House.

Andrews, E. D. (2016). *INTERPRETING THE BIBLE: Introduction to Biblical Hermeneutics.* Cambridge, OH: Christian Publishing House.

Andrews, E. D. (2016). *THE COMPLETE GUIDE to BIBLE TRANSLATION: Bible Translation Choices and Translation Principles [Second Edition]* . Cambridge: Christian Publishing House.

Andrews, E. D. (2016). *YOUR GUIDE FOR DEFENDING THE BIBLE: Self-Education of the Bible Made Easy.* Cambridge, OH: Christian Publishing House.

Andrews, E. D. (2016). *YOUR WORD IS TRUTH: Being Sanctified In the Truth.* Cambridge, OH: Christian Publishing House.

Andrews, E. D. (2018). *THE KING JAMES BIBLE: Do You Know the King James Version?* Cambridge, OH: Christian Publishing House.

Andrews, E. D. (2019). *400,000+ SCRIBAL ERRORS IN THE GREEK NEW TESTAMENT MANUSCRIPTS: What Assurance Do We Have that We Can Trust the Bible?* Cambridge, OH: Christian Publishing House.

Andrews, E. D. (2019). *INTRODUCTION TO THE TEXT OF THE NEW TESTAMENT: From The Authors and Scribe to the Modern Critical Text.* Cambridge, Ohio: Christian Publishing House.

Andrews, E. D. (2019). *THE READING CULTURE OF EARLY CHRISTIANITY: The Production, Publication, Circulation, and Use of Books in the Early Christian Church.* Cambridge, OH: Christian Publishing House.

Andrews, E. D. (2020). *INERRANCY OF SCRIPTURE: How Can We Believe Inerrancy of Scripture In the Originals When We Don't Have the Originals?* Cambridge, OH: Christian Publishing House.

Andrews, E. D. (2020). *THE NEW TESTAMENT DOCUMENTS: Can They Be Trusted?* Cambridge, OH: Christian Publishing House.

Andrews, E. D. (2020). *THE P52 PROJECT: Is P52 Really the Earliest Greek New Testament Manuscript?* Cambridge, OH: Christian Publishing House.

Andrews, E. D. (2022). *THE ORIGINAL TEXT OF THE NEW TESTAMENT: Ascertaining the Original Words of the Original Greek New Testament Manuscripts.* Cambridge, OH: Christian Publishing House.

Andrews, E. D. (2023). *A JOURNEY THROUGH ANCIENT LETTER WRITING: A New Look at New Testament Letters in the Greco-Roman World.* Cambridge, OH: Christian Publishing House.

Andrews, E. D. (2023). *BIBLICAL EXEGESIS: Biblical Criticism on Trial.* Cambridge, OH: Christian Publishing House.

Andrews, E. D. (2023). *CHRISTIAN APOLOGETICS: Answering the Tough Questions: Evidence and Reason in Defense of the Faith.* Cambridge, Ohio: Christian Publishing House.

Andrews, E. D. (2023). *DISCOVERING THE ORIGINAL BIBLE: Accuracy, Authenticity, and Reliability.* Cambridge, OH: Christian Publishing House.

Andrews, E. D. (2023). *GOD'S OUTLAW: William Tyndale and the English Bible.* Cambridge, Ohio: Christian Publishing House.

Andrews, E. D. (2023). *HOW WE GOT THE BIBLE.* Cambridge, OH: Christian Publishing House.

Andrews, E. D. (2023). *INTRODUCTION TO OLD TESTAMENT TEXTUAL CRITICISM.* Cambridge, OH: Christian Publishing House.

Andrews, E. D. (2023). *INTRODUCTION TO THE TEXT OF THE OLD TESTAMENT: From the Authors and Scribes to the Modern Critical Text.* Cambridge, OH: Christian Publishing House.

Andrews, E. D. (2023). *JOHN CALVIN: A Solitary Quest for the Truth.* Cambridge, Ohio: Christian Publishing House.

Andrews, E. D. (2023). *MARTIN LUTHER: The Man and His Legacy.* Cambridge, Ohio: Christian Publishing House.

Andrews, E. D. (2023). *THE BIBLE AS HISTORY: A Historical Journey Through the Bible.* Cambridge, Ohio: Christian Publishing House.

Andrews, E. D. (2023). *THE BIBLE ON TRIAL: Examining the Evidence for Being Inspired, Inerrant, Authentic, and True.* Cambridge, Ohio: Christian Publishing House.

Andrews, E. D. (2023). *THE NASB: Preserving Truth or Compromising Accuracy?: A Critical Look at the Shift from the 1995 to 2020 Editions of the New American Standard Bible (NASB).* Cambridge, OH: Christian Publishing House.

Andrews, E. D. (2023). *THE OLD TESTAMENT: Commentary, Background, & Bible Difficulties (Introduction to the Old Testament).* Cambridge, OH: Christian Publishing House.

Andrews, E. D. (2023). *THE SCRIBE AND THE TEXT OF THE NEW TESTAMENT: Scribal Activities in the Transmission of the*

Text of the New Testament. Cambridge, Ohio: Christian Publishing House.

Andrews, E. D. (2023). *THE TEXT OF THE NEW TESTAMENT: A Beginners Handbook to New Testament Textual Studies.* Cambridge, OH: Christian Publishing House.

Andrews, E. D. (2023). *THE TEXTUS RECEPTUS: The "Received Text" of the New Testament.* Cambridge, OH: Christian Publishing House.

Andrews, E. D. (2023). *Unlocking the Bible: A Beginner's Guide to the Coherence-Based Genealogical Method (CBGM): Understanding How Scholars Piece Together the New Testament.* Cambridge, OH: Christian Publishing House.

Andrews, E. D. (2024). *DO WE STILL NEED A LITERAL BIBLE?: Discover the Truth about Literal Bibles.* Cambridge, OH: Christian Publishing House.

Andrews, E. D. (2024). *INTRODUCTION TO HANDWRITING STYLES: Authenticating and Dating New Testament Manuscripts.* Cambridge, OH: Christian Publishing House.

Andrews, E. D. (2025). *BIBLICAL WORDS AND THEIR MEANING: An Introduction to Lexical Semantics.* Cambridge, OH: Christian Publishing House.

Andrews, E. D. (2025). *CAN WE TRUST THE BIBLE?* Cambridge, OH: Christian Publishing House.

Andrews, E. D. (2025). *LINGUISTICS AND THE BIBLICAL TEXT: Unlocking Scripture Through the Science of Language.* Cambridge, OH: Christian Publishing House.

Andrews, E. D. (2025). *THE ANDREWS BIBLE BLUEPRINT: Unlocking Scripture's Truth, History, and Wisdom.* Cambridge, OH: Christian Publishing House.

Andrews, E. D. (2025). *THE EARLY VERSIONS OF THE NEW TESTAMENT: Their Origins, Transmission, and Reliability.* Cambridge, OH: Christian Publishing House.

Andrews, E. D. (2025). *THE ENCYCLOPEDIA OF THE TEXT OF THE NEW TESTAMENT: The Resource for Pastors, Teachers, and Believers.* Cambridge, OH: Christian Publishing House.

Andrews, E. D. (2025). *UNDERSTANDING BIBLICAL WORDS: A Guide to Sound Interpretation.* Cambridge, OH: Christian Publishing House.

Andrews, E. D., & Farnell, F. D. (2017). *BIBLICAL CRITICISM: What are Some Outstanding Weaknesses of Modern Historical Criticism?* Cambridge, OH: Christian Publishing House.

Archer, G. L. (1982). *Encyclopedia of Bible Difficulties.* Grand Rapids: Zondervan.

Archer, G. L. (1994). *A Survey of Old Testament Introduction.* Chicago: Moody.

Arduini, S., & Hodgson Jr., R. (2004). *Similarities and Differences in Translation.* New York: American Bible Society.

Arndt, W., Danker, F. W., & Bauer, W. (2000). *A Greek-English Lexicon of the New Testament and Other Early Christian Literature. 3rd ed. .* Chicago: University of Chicago Press.

Baer, D. (2007). *The Unquenchable Fire.* Maitland, FL: Xulon Press.

Barnett, P. (2005). *The Birth of Christianity: The First Twenty Years (After Jesus, Vol. 1) .* Grand Rapids, MI: Wm. B. Eerdmans .

Barnwell, K. (1974). *Introduction to Semantics and Translation.* England: SIL.

Barnwell, K. (1975). *Bible Translation: An Introductory Course in Translation Principles.* Kenya: SIL International.

Beekman, J., & Callow, J. (1974). *Translating the Word of God.* Grand Rapids: Zondervan.

Bercot, D. W. (1998). *A Dictionary of Early Christian Beliefs.* Peabody: Hendrickson.

Bock, D. L. (2006). *The Missing Gospels: Unerthing the Truth Behind Alternative Christianities.* Nashville, TN: Thomas Nelson.

Bock, D. L., & Wallace, D. B. (2007). *Dethroning Jesus: Exposing Popular Culture's Quest to Unseat the Biblical Christ.* Nashville: Thomas Nelson.

Borgen, P. (1997). *Philo of Alexandria: An Exegete for His Time.* Leiden, Boston: Brill.

Brand, C., Draper, C., & Archie, E. (2003). *Holman Illustrated Bible Dictionary: Revised, Updated and Expanded.* Nashville, TN: Holman.

Bruce, F. F. (1981). *The New Testament Documents: Are they Reliable?* Downer Groves: Inter Varsity. Retrieved April 03, 2009, from Institute for Study of Ancient Manuscripts: http://www.libertyparkusafd.org/lp/Burgon/cd-roms/121bible.html

Bruce, F. F., Packer, J. I., Cmfort, P., & Henry, C. F. (1992, 2003). *The Origin of the Bible.* Carol Steam, IL: Tyndale House.

Comfort, P. (2005). *Encounterring the Manuscripts: An Introduction to New Testament Paleography and Textual Criticism.* Nashville: Broadman & Holman.

Comfort, P. W. (1992). *Early Manuscripts & Modern Translations of the New Testament.* Wheaton, IL: Tyndale House Publishers.

Comfort, P. W. (1992). *The Quest for the Original Text of the New Testament.* Eugene, Oregon: Wipf and Stock Publishers.

Comfort, P. W. (1992). *The Quest for the Original Text of the New Testament.* Eugene: Wipf and Stock.

Comfort, P. W. (2000). *Essential Guide to Bible Versions.* Wheaton: Tyndale House.

Comfort, P. W. (2005). *ENCOUNTERING THE MANUSCRIPTS: An Introduction to New Testament Paleography and Textual Criticism.* Nashville, TN: Broadman & Holman.

Comfort, P. W. (2008). *New Testament Text and Translation Commentary.* Carol Stream, IL: Tyndale House Publishers.

Comfort, P. W. (2008). *New Testament Text and Translation Commentary.* Carol Stream: Tyndale House Publishers.

Comfort, P. W. (2008). *New Testament Text and Translation Commentary: Commentary on the Variant Readings of the Ancient New Testament Manuscripts and How They Relate to the Major English Translations.* Carol Stream, IL: Tyndale House Publishers.

Comfort, P., & Barret, D. (2001). *The Text of the Earliest New Testament Greek Manuscripts.* Wheaton: Tyndale House Publishers.

Comfort, P., & Barret, D. (2019). *THE TEXT OF THE EARLIEST NEW TESTAMENT MANUSCRIPTS: Papyri 1-72, Vol. 1 .* Grand Rapids, MI: Kregel Academic.

Comfort, P., & Barret, D. (2019). *THE TEXT OF THE EARLIEST NEW TESTAMENT MANUSCRIPTS: Papyri 75-139 and Uncials, Vol. 2.* Grand Rapids, MI: Kregel Academic.

Cruse, C. F. (1998). *Eusebius' Eccliatical History.* Peabody, MA: Hendrickson.

Dever, W. G. (2001). *What Did the Biblical Writers Know, and When Did They Know It?* Grand Rapids: William B. Eerdmans Publishing Company.

Dewey, D. (2004). *A User's Guide to Bible Translation: Making the Most of Different Versions.* Downers Grove : InterVaristy Press.

Durant, W. &. (1950). *The Story of Civilization: Part IV—The Age of Faith.* New York, NY: Simon & Schuster.

Edwards, T. (1908). *A Dictionary of Thoughts.* Detroit: F. B. Dickerson Company.

Ehrman, B. D. (1995). *The Text of the New Testament in Contemporary Research: Essays on the Status Quaestionis .* Grand Rapids, MI: Eerdmans.

Ehrman, B. D. (2003). *Lost Christianities: The Battles for Scripture and the Faiths We Never Knew .* New York: Oxford University Press.

Ehrman, B. D. (2005). *Misquoting Jesus: The Story Behind Who Changed the Bible and Why.* New York: Harper One.

Elwell, W. A. (2001). *Evangelical Dictionary of Theology (Second Edition)*. Grand Rapids: Baker Academic.

Elwell, W. A., & Comfort, P. W. (2001). *Tyndale Bible Dictionary*. Wheaton, Ill: Tyndale House Publishers.

Evans, C. A. (2002). *Fabricating Jesus: How Modern Scholars Distort the Gospels*. Downers Grove, IL: InterVaristy Press.

F. Garcia Martinez, J. B., Martinez, F. G., & Barrera, J. T. (1995). *The People of the Dead Sea Scrolls: Their Writings, Beliefs and Practices*. Leiden: Brill Academic.

Ferguson, E. (2003). *Backgrounds of Early Christianity*. Grand Rapids, MI: Wm. B. Eerdmans.

Gamble, H. Y. (1995). *Books and Readers in the Early Church: A History of Early Christian Texts*. New Haven: New Haven University Press.

Geisler, N. L. (1980). *Inerrancy*. Grand Rapids, MI: Zondervan.

Geisler, N. L. (1981). *Biblical Errancy: An Analysis of Its Philosophical Roots*. Eugene, OR: Wipf and Stock Publisher.

Geisler, N. L. (2007). *A Popular Survey of the New Testament*. Grand Rapids: Baker Books.

Geisler, N. L. (2012). *Defending Inerrancy: Affirming the Accuracy of Scripture for a New Generation*. Grand Rapids, MI: Baker Books.

Geisler, N. L., & Howe, T. (1992). *The Big Book of Bible Difficulties*. Grand Rapids: Baker Books.

Geisler, N. L., & Nix, W. E. (1996). *A General Introduction to the Bible*. Chicago: Moody Press.

Green, J. B., McKnight, S., & Marshall, H. (1992). *Dictionary of Jesus and the Gospels*. Downers Grove, IL: InterVarsity Press.

Greenlee, J. H. (1995). *Introduction to New Testament Textual Criticism*. Peabody: Hendrickson.

Greenlee, J. H. (2008). *Introduction to New Testament Textual Criticism (Revised ed.)*. Peabody, MA: Hendrickson Publishers.

Greenlee, J. H. (2012). *The Text of the New Testament: From Manuscript to Modern Edition.* Grand Rapids, MI: Baker Academic.

Grudem, W., Ryken, L., Collins, J. C., Poythress, V. S., & Winter, B. (2005). *Translating Truth: The Case for Essentially Literal Bible Translation.* Wheaton: Crossway Books.

Hodges, Z. &. (1985). *The Greek New Testament According to the Majority Text.* Nashville, TN: Thomas Nelson Publishers.

Hoffman, J. M. (2007). *AND GOD SAID: How Translations Conceal the Bible's Original Meaning.* New York, NY: Thomas Dunne Books.

Holmes, M. W. (2007). *The Apostolic Fathers: Greek Texts and English Translations.* Grand Rapids: Baker Academics.

Hurtado, L. W. (2006). *The Earliest Christian Artifacts: Manuscripts and Christian Origins.* Grand Rapids: Eerdmans.

Hurtado, L. W. (2019). *TEXTS AND ARTIFACTS: Selected Essays on Textual Criticism ans Early Christian Manuscripts.* New York, NY: T & T Clark.

James, M. R. (1924, 2004). *The Apocryphal New Testament.* Berkeley, CA: Apocryphile Press.

Johnson, W. A., & Parker, H. N. (2011). *Ancient Literacies: The Culture of Reading in Greece and Rome.* Oxford: Oxford University Press.

Jones, T. P. (2007). *Misquoting Truth: A Guide to the Fallacies of Bart Ehrman's Misquoting Jesus.* Downer Groves: InterVarsity Press.

Kaiser, W. C., Davids, P. H., & Bruce, F. F. (1996). *Hard Sayings of the Bible.* Downer Groves, IL: Inter Varsity Press.

Keener, C. S. (1993). *The IVP Bible Background Commentary: New Testament.* Downer Groves, IL: InterVarsity Press.

Kenyon, F. G. (2006). *The Palaeography of Greek Papyri.* Whitefish: Kessinger Publishing.

Kistemaker, S. J., & Hendriksen, W. (1953-2001). *New Testament Commentary: Exposition of the Acts of the Apostles .* Grand Rapids, MI: Baker Book House.

Komoszewski, J. E., M. Sawyer, J., & Wallace, D. (2006). *Reinventing Jesus*. Grand Rapids, MI: Kregel Publications.

Lightfoot, N. R. (1963, 1988, 2003). *How We Got the Bible*. Grand Rapids, MI: Baker Books.

Lindsell, H. (1976). *The Battle for the Bible*. Grand Rapids: Zondervan.

Linnemann. (1992). *Is There A Synoptic Problem? Rethinking the Literary Dependance of the First Three Gospels*. Grand Rapids, MI: Baker Book House.

Linnemann, E. (2001). *Biblical Criticism on Trial: How Scientific is "Scientific Theology"?* Grand Rapids: Kregel.

McDonald, L. M. (July 13, 2009). *Forgotten Scriptures: The Selection and Rejection of Early Religious Writings*. Louisville: Westminster John Knox Press.

Metzger, B. (2001). *The Bible in Translation: Ancient and English Versions*. Grand Rapids: Baker Academic.

Metzger, B. M. (1964, 1968, 1992). *The Text of the New Testament: Its Transmission, Corruption, and Transmission*. New York: Oxford University Press.

Metzger, B. M. (1994). *A Textual Commentary on the Greek New Testament*. New York: United Bible Society.

Metzger, B. M. (1994). *A Textual Commentary on the Greek New Testament (2nd ed.)*. New York: United Bible Society.

Metzger, B. M., & Ehrman, B. D. (2005). *The Text of the New Testament: Its Transmission, Corruption, and Restoration (4th Edition)*. New York: Oxford University Press.

Milligan, G. (2009). *The New Testament Documents, Their Origin and Early History*. New York, NY: General Books LLC.

Mounce, W. D. (2006). *Mounce's Complete Expository Dictionary of Old & New Testament Words*. Grand Rapids, MI: Zondervan.

Munday, J. (2009). *Introducing Translation Studies: Theories and Applications (2bd Edition)*. London: Routledge.

Oates, J. F., Samuel, A. E., & Welles, B. C. (1967). *Yale Papyri in the Beinecke Rare Book and Manuscript Library* . (New Haven: American Society of Papyrologists.

Orchard, B. (1776-1976, 2005). *J. J. Griesbach: Synoptic and Text - Critical Studies* . Cambridge: Cambridge University Press.

Packer, J. I. (1965). *God Speaks to Man: Revelation and the Bible.* Atlanta: Westminster Press.

Pagels, E. (1989). *The Gnostic Gospels.* New York: Vintage.

Parker, D. C. (1997). *The living Text of the Gospels.* Cambridge: Cambridge University Press.

Pickering, W. (1980). *The Identity of the New Testament Text (rev. ed.).* Nashville: Nelson.

Porter, S. E. (2013). *HOW WE GOT THE NEW TESTAMENT: Text, Transmission, Translation.* Grand Tapids, MI: Baker Academic.

Porter, S. E., & Boda, M. J. (2009). *Translating the New Testament.* Grand Rapids, MI: Wm. B. Eerdmans.

Porter, S. E., & Hess, R. S. (2004). *Translating the Bible: Problems and Prospects.* New York, NY: T&T Clark International.

Poythress, V. S. (2004). *The TNIV and The Gender-Neutral Bible Controversy.* Nashville: Boardman & Holman.

Price, R. (2007). *Searching for the Original Bible.* Eugene: Harvest House.

Ray, V. (1982). The Formal vs Dynamic Equivalent Principle in New Testament Translation. *Restoration Quarterly 25*, 46-56.

Rhodes, R. (2009). *The Complete Guid to Bible Translations.* Eugene, OR: Harvest House.

Richards, E. R. (2004). *Paul And First-Century Letter Writing: Secretaries, Composition and Collection.* Downers Grove: InterVarsity Press.

Roberts, A., & Donaldson, J. (1994). *The Ante-Nicene Fathers.* Peabody: Hendrickson.

Roberts, C. H. (1970). *Books in the Graeco-Roman World and in the New Testament in the Cambridge History of the Bible, Vol. 1, From the Beginnings to Jerome* . Cambridge: Cambridge University Press.

Roberts, C. H. (1979). *Manuscript, Society, and Belief in Early Christian Egypt.* London: Oxford University Press.

Roberts, C. H., & Skeat, T. C. (1987). *The Birth of the Codex.* London: Oxford University Press.

Robertson, A. T. (1925). *An Introduction to the Textual Criticism of the New Testament.* London: Hodder & Stoughton.

Ryken, L. (2002). *The Word of God in English.* Wheaton: Crossway Books.

Ryken, L. (2005). *Choosing a Bible: Understanding Bible Translation Differences.* Wheaton: Crossway Books.

Ryken, L. (2009). *Understanding English Bible Translation: The Case for an Essentially Literal Approach.* Wheaton, IL: Crossway Books.

Schurer, E. (1890). *A HISTORY OF THE JEWISH PEOPLE IN THE TIME OF JESUS CHRIST (Volume II).* Edinburgh: T. & T. Clark.

Scorgie, G. G., Strauss, M. L., & Voth, S. M. (2003). *The Challenge of Bible Translation.* Grand Rapids: Zondervan.

Scott, J. J. (1995). *Jewish Backgrounds of the New Testament.* Grand Rapids, MI: Baker Academic.

Souter, A. (1913). *The Text and Canon of the New Testament.* New York: Charles Scribner's Sons.

Sturz, H. A. (1984). *The Byzantine Text-Type & New Testament Textual Criticism.* Nashville, TN: Thomas Nelson Publishers.

Thomas, R. L. (2000). *How to Choose a Bible Version.* Scotland: Christian Focus Publications.

Thomas, R. L. (2002). *Three Views of the Origins of the Synoptic Gospels.* Grand Rapids, MI: Kregel.

Thomas, R. L., & Farnell, F. D. (1998). *THE JESUS CRISIS: The Inroads of Historical Criticism in Evagelical Scholarship.* Grand Rapids, MI: Kregel Publications.

Torrey, R. A. (1907). *Difficulties in the Bible: Alleged Errors and Contradictions.* Chicago: Moody Press.

University, S. (2012). *Calculating the Time and Cost of Paul's Missionary Journeys.* Retrieved 07 12, 2014, from http://www.openbible.info/blog/2012/07/calculating-the-time-and-cost-of-pauls-missionary-journeys/

Vine, W. E. (1996). *Vine's Expository Dictionary of Old and New Testament Words.* Nashville: Thomas Nelson.

Virkler, H. A., & Ayayo, K. G. (1981, 2007). *Hermeneutics: Principles and Processes of Biblical Interpretation.* Grand Rapids, MI: Baker Academic.

Wallace, D. (2011). *The Reliability of the New Testament: Bart Ehrman and Daniel Wallace in Dialogue.* Minneapolis, MN: Fortress Press.

Wallace, D. B. (2008, Winter). *bible.org.* Retrieved December 18, 2011, from http://bible.org/article/number-textual-variants-evangelical-miscalculation

Wallace, D. B. (2011). *Revisiting the Corruption of the New Testament: Manuscript, Patristic, and Apocryphal Evidence.* Grand Rapids, MI: Kregel Publications.

Walton, J. H., Matthews, V. H., & Chavalas, M. W. (2000). *The IVP Bible Background Commentary: Old Testament.* Downers Grove: IVP Academic.

Wasserman, T. &. (2017). *A New Approach to Textual Criticism: An Introduction to the Coherence-Based Genealogical Method.* Atlanta: SBL Press.

Wegner, P. D. (2006). *A Student's Guide to Textual Criticism of the Bible: Its History Methods & Results.* Downers Grove: InterVarsity Press.

Westcott, B. F., & A., H. F. (1882). *The New Testament in the Original Greek, Vol. 2: Introduction, Appendix.* London: Macmillan and Co.

Westcott, B. F., & Hort, F. J. (1882). *Introduction to the New Testament in the Original Greek: Appendix.* New York, NY: Harper and Brothers.

Whiston, W. (1987). *The Works of Josephus.* Peabody, MA: Hendrickson.

www.ingramcontent.com/pod-product-compliance
Lightning Source LLC
LaVergne TN
LVHW020930090426
835512LV00020B/3295